# A Couple of Nobodies from Nowhere

By
Paul E. Portman

Goose Flats Publishing ~ Tombstone, Arizona

# A Couple of Nobodies from Nowhere
## By Paul E. Portman

Copyright © 2019 by Paul E. Portman
ISBN # 978-1-939345-26-4
Library of Congress Control Number: 2019954464

Published and printed in the U.S.A.

First printing December 2019

Published for Paul E. Portman by
Goose Flats Graphics & Publishing
P.O. Box 813
Tombstone, Arizona 85638
(520) 457-3884
www.gooseflats.com

Book layout & cover design:
Keith Davis
Goose Flats Graphics & Publishing
Tombstone, Arizona

# Table of Contents

A Couple of Nobodies...

Thanks to:

Julia Todd

Emerald Pen

My Brother John

Janice Hendricks

"Everyone has the ability to change.
I know I did."

# February 1980

I was sitting in the living room of the Player Agent for San Diego's Balboa Junior Baseball League surrounded by her fellow board members. I was ready to answer any questions they may ask. This was, after all, a requirement to coach my son Phil's baseball team.

In early January, I registered my five-year-old son to play in the local baseball league. I thought this would be a good opportunity for him and me to spend time together while getting to know other like-minded people in our community.

The league's registration form, asked the question, "Would you like to volunteer to coach a team?" I checked the box, yes. A week later, I received a call from the president of the league inviting me to their monthly board meeting. He told me that I would have to be approved as a coach by the league's Board of Directors and, would I be able to make it to their next board meeting. I gladly said, yes. Because I had only arrived in California from Pennsylvania a few months earlier and didn't know any of the people in the room, I felt nervous. Also, I didn't have any local references or previous coaching experience. Other than that, I was excited about meeting people with a common purpose.

As the interview commenced, I fielded their questions as if I was Mike Schmidt fielding hot grounders for the Philadelphia Phillies. The first question was from the league President.

"Do you have time to attend all the games and practices?"

"Yes."

The next question was from the Field Coordinator.

"Will you be able to attend all the field maintenance events and cut the grass when it's your turn?"

"Yes."

I'm thinking this is easy; I got it made. Then, the Official Score Keeper hit me with a tough question.

"Do you ever use foul language?"

In my head, I ask myself, "What the hell is this dumb ass worried about? Is she a holy roller or what?"

She must have seen the perplexed look on my face because she said, "Last season we had a coach curse a child for misbehaving in the dug-out."

I told her that I work in a shipyard and hear and use bad language, but I don't bring my work home with me.

"Any more questions for Mr. Webster?" the president asked.

Everyone politely shook their head no, and he concluded the interview.

I began to relax as the player agent served cookies and soft drinks. The conversation became casual as we sat and ate her cookies. I never felt at ease speaking around strangers, so I was proud of myself for the way I handled this situation. I knew if I stayed relaxed everything would be fine. That's when the player agent asked what should have been the easiest question of the evening.

"Mr. Webster, what brought you and your family to San Diego? Were you in the Navy?"

I was stunned, my mouth opened and as I inhaled my jaw dropped, my thumb started to massage the tip of my middle finger, and I was speechless. I was thinking to myself, "You fucking dummy. What the hell did you get yourself into now? You should have rehearsed a response to this question!" I took a sip of iced tea. It was only two seconds but seemed longer when I replied, as composed as I could.

"No, I was never in the service. My wife and I just needed to get away." ॐ

## Chapter 1 - Nowheresville

In the late 1950s, I was living in Driftwood, Pennsylvania. Driftwood is part of Lower Manchester Township. It's located in the southeast corner of Pennsylvania in Delaware County. North of Driftwood is Castleton, a third-class city. Castleton is about five miles from the Philadelphia City limits. Most of Castleton and all Lower Manchester Township are occupied by blue-collar middle-class folks. Most have lived there for generations and know everyone in their own neighborhood. The neighborhood I lived in was no different than many others around Philadelphia.

The area is dominated in both size and employment by two oil refineries; Sinclair and Sun Oil. Our modest house sat on the corner of Cole and Claremont Streets within ear and eye range of the Sun Oil refinery. Our house was built around the turn of the 20th century and is a single-standing, wood-framed two-story house. The house has three bedrooms and one bathroom, a cellar and no attic. The front has a large weeping willow tree on the Claremont Street side of the front yard. In the spring and summer, the willow tree provided shade and thankfully, blocked the view to Sun Oil. Behind the house was a garage, but we never used it for the car; just the push lawn mower, some garden tools, and old junk. My dad's family, the Webster's, are third-generation Americans of German and English descent and were raised Episcopalian, My dad and his siblings were raised in this house.

In 1935, when my father was 16-years-old, his father passed away. Since he was the eldest of the six Webster's, he took over as the head of the household. My father's name is James, and he had two brothers, Philip, and John, whom everyone called Jack. He also had three sisters, Katherine, Delores, and Mary.

My mother's name is Dorothy and she lived just a half of a block down Claremont Street from the Webster's with her parents, Joe and Eleanor Quinn. Mom was an only child. Her family is three parts Irish and one part German. My father, James, and my mother, Dorothy, fell in love and married when he was twenty and she was eighteen years old. They moved into a nearby apartment and started their family. Things remained this way until all of my paternal aunts and uncles left home. When my Grandmother Webster moved in with my Uncle Jack my parents moved back into the house on Cole Street where dad grew up. By then, my two oldest sisters, Elizabeth and Ann, were born.

My parents both had calm dispositions and, for the most part, got along pretty well. Years later, I would hear my father call my mother by her pet name, Quinny. My father resembled a combination of Henry Fonda and Ward Cleaver and my mother's looks reminded me of a cross between Pearl Bailey and Elizabeth Taylor. Neither of my parents' families had any money to speak of. My mom's father hardly worked.  I didn't find out he didn't work until I was an adult and I didn't ask why. Pop Pop Quinn passed away when I was around seven years old. My maternal grandmother "Nana" was the breadwinner. My mom would tell stories of how in her early teens Nana would send her to live with her father's sister, Aunt Alice, in Winter Gardens, Florida. My mother occasionally recalled fond memories of her time in Florida.

The Quinns were Roman Catholic. Before my parents married, my father converted to Catholicism. In recollection, I have fond memories of my childhood years. I remember going down Claremont Street after church on Sundays to have breakfast at Nana and Pop Pop Quinn's house. I especially remember the time when my brothers and I were behaving badly. Pop Pop Quinn said he was going to beat us with his belt but when he loosened his belt his pants began to fall down. Luckily, we were able to escape his punishment by outrunning him. I guess my brothers and I wore out our welcome that day. Pop Pop had little tolerance for children. That may be why my mother was an only child.

Most of the people living on Cole or Claremont Street were Irish, German, or Scotch-Americans and most were Catholic or Protestant, with a few first-generation Italian-Americans mixed in. Most everyone belonged to nearby Holy Sacrament Church and most of the men worked at Sun Oil Refinery. Driftwood was a close neighborhood with a population density of about four thousand people per square mile. Most people's world was confined to either Driftwood, Penn's Port, or nearby Castleton. In those days, a person needed to go to Castleton for the things that you couldn't get in Sunny's General Store or Jones's Drug Store in Driftwood. The Red Arrow bus line would pass our house a few times every weekday. You could just hop on the bus to go clothes shopping or attend the movie theater in Castleton.

My mother's maternal uncles were successful men. Peter was a Parish priest and Uncle Daniel retired as a Brigadier General in the Army Reserve and Uncle Joe was a businessman in nearby Wilmington, Delaware. My mother did not have much of a relationship with them. They were hard workers and rumor has it that mom's uncles were not fond of Pop Pop Quinn because he didn't have a steady job.

My mother yearned for her relatives. She always spoke kindly of her cousin Eddie Doyle out in California and would send Christmas cards to him and her Aunt Alice in Florida. When my older brothers returned from military duty in the Far East my mother would make sure they stopped in California to see Cousin Eddie near San Francisco.

Although she didn't have money, my mother was able to create wealth in another way. She and my father made babies, 11 of them to be exact. Now, I have to say, being the seventh of eleven children wasn't bad. As a matter of fact, that's my version of heaven. My mother was able to show love for every one of us. There has to be something said for a woman who wants eleven children. I don't mean just *wants*; I mean *loves* every one of us, and *lets us know it*. There were times when I thought I was her only child.

Typically in Driftwood, no one had anything more than a high school education and that suited my parent's generation just fine. That also suited Sun Oil employment requirements. Everyone around here knew if a man got a job at Sun Oil he had it made. My father worked as a laborer for Sun Oil from the age of eighteen. He worked the day shift which allowed him to come home for lunch and he was always home at night for the family. He kept in touch with his friends and sometimes they would come over to watch the Friday night fights on the television. In the summer, dad's friends would stop by and sit in the shade under the willow tree in the front yard or come up and sit on the porch and talk and hang out. A couple of my father's friends smoked cigarettes and drank a little beer, but they were never out of control. It seemed odd to me that my father would refer to his group of friends as "the gang."

Every year, my family would take a vacation. In 1959, we went to Disneyland in California. On our way, we saw the Painted Desert, Petrified Forest, and the Grand Canyon.

In 1960, we took a drive down to visit the city of New Orleans, this is where I did my Houdini act; let me explain, after riding in the car for an entire day my brothers and I ran into the motel room and started jumping on the bed. I am not sure how it happened but I ended up hitting my head on the bed's wooden headboard and splitting my head open. I was rushed to the hospital by ambulance and put in the emergency room. The next thing I remember was that I was struggling to get out of a straight jacket and showing my mom, "Look, Mom, one hand!" As I was loosening the other arm the doctor stuck a needle in my shoulder and I was out. The next thing I remember was that we were on the road to Fort Lauderdale, Florida. We stayed there for a few days before returning home.

We even traveled to Niagara Falls in New York and then over into Canada in 1961. The whole family, eight or nine of us by then, would hop in our powder blue 1955 Ford station wagon with the luggage on the roof and we would be on our way. The eldest were three girls: Elizabeth, Ann, and Katherine. Next came four boys: James Jr., John, Gerald, and me. We were followed by two more girls: Mary and Joan. Kevin our youngest brother may have been born at this time, but I forget, and I know for sure that the baby girl of the family, Ruth, wasn't around during those times. Like my parents, we all enjoyed average good looks, not Hollywood good looks, except maybe Ann (more on that later), but above average for small town Driftwood "good looks." We could go pretty far from Cole Street and have someone say, "You must be a Webster, I can tell by your eyes." We all had blue eyes, some deeper blue than others. Our dark eyebrows brought even more attention to this feature. Elizabeth, Katherine, John, and Ruth had dark brown hair; Gerald, me, Mary, and Kevin had medium brown hair, while Ann, Jimmy, and Joan had light brown hair. It seemed wherever we went in Driftwood our family's fine reputation preceded us.

Sometimes my mother would send a couple of us boys up to the local pharmacy or grocery store. When we went we would always go in pairs, not because it was a bad area or anything like that, it was just to keep each other company. Or perhaps my mother didn't want anyone to think they were singled out to go and run an errand. Sometimes the older guys hanging on the corner would say random stuff to us. Once, when we went to the Acme Market, one guy said to his buddies, "Hey, what's the meaning of the word serendipity?" Another would say, "I don't know. Let's ask the Webster dictionary boys."

That was kind of cool because we knew they were just messing around. I think they liked my sister Ann and were just trying to be weird to her younger brothers. The fact that you have a good looking older sister and a family with an honest reputation made my childhood easy. The only time I was afraid was when my older brothers, James or John, would tease me about someone hiding in the closet or some nerd was after me for laughing at him. We were kind of bad like that.

When I was in the fifth grade I played for Holy Sacrament's basketball team. We played in the Castleton Catholic Youth Organization (CCYO). I also played Little League Baseball. In those days, you had to be at least eight years old and try out before joining the league. If you weren't good enough, you were not chosen by the coach and you did not get on a team. Not like today where everyone who signs up gets on a team.

Our little league was average in size with eight teams total; four Minor League teams composed of 8 through 12-year-olds and the Major League for ten to twelve years old with more talent. Starting at age 8 I played two years in the minors and three years in the majors. Our league was named after a local guy from Penn's Port named James "Mickey" Vernon. He played professional baseball for the Washington Senators. Each year around October, our league would have a banquet to celebrate the past season. Mickey would give his speech to the attendees of the banquet and, once when my dad was there, Mickey came by to speak to him and this made me feel special.

I played sports whenever I had a chance. I was comfortable while playing sports because I have good hand and eye coordination, quick reflexes, and even though I was skinny, I was strong. Sports helped balance my self-esteem and took my mind off of school, at which I wasn't good. Playing a team sport made me feel special when I was able to accomplish things that would help my team win. Even if my team doesn't win the game I enjoy the competition. Winning a game against weak competition has little value to me. I would rather play well and lose against a superior opponent. Most of the time before I play in a game I go over in my mind different scenarios where I see myself either hitting, catching or throwing a ball to make an outstanding play. And, when I do it in real time, I feel as if I am accomplishing something. As an added bonus I was getting out a little aggression and this makes my spare time more enjoyable. My father didn't play on any teams when he was younger but showed some interest when I did. My older sisters danced and sang. Once they even tap danced for a radio program. I remember they would go to dancing school with Aunt Mary. Later, my younger sisters, Mary and Joan, would attend the same dancing school.

When I was twelve, some of the boys in the neighborhood played organized football in Upper Manchester. My older brother, Gerald, and I thought we had what it took so we joined them. We were on different teams because the teams were separated by weight and age. Gerald weighed about ten pounds more than me at the time. I didn't appreciate the sport very much. I was good enough at the game, but you have to physically dominate your opponent in order to succeed. This strategy was unlike baseball where your opponent, the pitcher, is at a distance and throws the ball past a plate. If the pitcher can't throw the ball across the plate and you can control yourself by not swinging at the ball you get to walk to first base. If you do hit the ball you go around him. Not that I'm a wimp or anything; because growing up in Lower Manchester Township you had to learn how to defend yourself. As well adjusted as working class people were, some of us picked on people who wouldn't fight back. I just wasn't fond of shoving someone around for the sport of it. The other reason I didn't like football was the way our coaches berated you with belittling language in an effort to psych you up to play. I did not respond well to this strategy. This behavior from the coaches made me want to get away from them and not accomplish their demands.

Besides my siblings, the neighborhood was full of kids to play with. Timmy Howard was our closest neighbor. He lived across the street and was less than a year younger than me. The Howards and the Websters were pretty close. Timmy's father died when he was three and his mother never remarried. He was the only boy and with four older sisters, all living with their widowed mother and grandmother.

If Tim wanted to hang out with males, he came to our house. Behind us lived the Laws; they had three sons. Their house was typical for the surrounding blocks. It was made of red brick and was a rectangle semi-detached house. Like the Laws, a lot of families on the block had a fancy first initial of their last names on metal screen doors. They all had a small back yard connected to each other; some were separated by a four-foot-high chain link fence, others by a row of hedges. These homes faced Claremont Street. There were about ten sets of them. They were filled with families by the names of Walklett, Jackson, Johnson, Adams, O'Conner, McKenna, Ceritella and Fusco. Each of those families had about three kids, and of course, they either went to Holy Sacrament School or their dads worked at Sun Oil or both.

Since the yards were small we mostly played in the streets. We played tag football or curb baseball. Curb baseball is played in the street by two people. One player throws a solid rubber ball about the size of a baseball against the corner of the curb. His opponent stands on the other side of the street and tries to catch the ball before it gets to the other curb. We always played in front of our house. This game was a good way to spend time and practice your throwing and catching skills.

On summer nights before the eleven o'clock curfew, we would play "Release." The teams were usually chosen by my brother Jimmy and our neighbor Paulie Walklett. One team would cover their eyes and the other would go and hide. Mostly about six or seven kids on a team. It's like hide and seek except once you are caught, they bring you back to home base, which was always the telephone pole on the corner of Cole and Claremont Streets. When caught your teammate can touch you before the other team touches them you are "released" and able to run and hide again. Some guys are able to make this last all night. These were good times. ✑

## Chapter 2 - Family First

Inside the Webster's house was just as easy going as what people saw on the outside. Mom didn't have a mean bone in her body and Dad kept things pretty mellow when he was around. Our home had an open porch set back from the public sidewalk by about twenty feet. The porch is accessed by a walkway, splitting the front yard and four cement steps to bring you to the level of the wooden porch. The porch roof is supported by three roman style wooden columns. Our entrance was plain. It consisted of a wooden screen door in front, no fancy initial, and a big white wooden door that had a small window. All the windows in the house had green trim and sometimes at night, it looked pretty nice.

As you enter the house there was a hallway and immediately to the right were the steps to upstairs. No outsiders ever went upstairs. No particular reason -that was just the rule. I remember one time when my mother and father were both away; Nana was watching us she had to call Uncle Jack to come over to discipline us boys for not behaving. When Uncle Jack arrived we hid upstairs thinking we were safe. We began worrying when our brother John reminded us that Uncle Jack grew up in that same house and knew all the best hiding places. But, as it turned out, he knew his boundaries, he only bluffed coming up by placing his foot on the bottom step. He stopped and hollered up to us that we were going to get in trouble when we came down. He left after we were quiet for a while. All Nana wanted us to do was stop running around like a bunch of wild hooligans.

Our house was old but clean. As our numbers grew, we adapted to that old house and became a close family and this suited us well. The only vent for the heating furnace was in the hallway between the front door and the kitchen. This thing was a 3-foot by 3-foot black hole covered by black metal grating that allowed the hot air to come up from the furnace in the cellar and warm the entire house. After stepping into the hallway, to the left was the living room. Mom bought some beige colored furniture and painted the walls brown, about the color of a Hershey bar, and we had a beige television this was home central.

From there if you made a turn to the right you'd be in the dining room. On holidays we had big dinners there, but mostly the dining room was used to play board games, cards, and jacks. My brothers and sisters also used it to do their homework. In years gone by, a door separated each room, but soon there were only reminders of where the hinges were attached to the doorframe. When passing through, you could see markings of our heights as we grew through the years. Another right turn and you were in the kitchen. A table was there so we could sit down and eat, but it only has room for about six people at a time. On special occasions, we would clear off the dining room table and insert the leaf to enlarge the length of the table. We would slide six-inch wide boards across the three chairs on each side of the table and throw a towel on them to provide four extra sitting places. We kept the washing machine and ironing board in the kitchen too. The kitchen had a back door but we rarely used it. Out the back door was a shed with winter coats and boots, a couple of sleds, and assorted accumulated junk. Upstairs, the girls had the front bedroom. This was the largest of the bedrooms, covering the entire width of the second floor. The boys had the back bedroom, sharing the back width of the house with the bathroom. Mom and Dad had the middle room, leaving just a small area at the top of the steps for the hall.

We all did some work around the house, but mostly the girls did the cleaning. The boys cut the grass and were responsible to take out the trash and clean our own room. James, John, Gerald and I shared the boys' room using two sets of bunk beds. To this day, I don't remember where Kevin slept. Since we were left to our own, we mostly just cleaned up after ourselves. It seemed at least once a year there would be spring-cleaning. That is when mom would come and literally clean house from top to bottom. Other than that the standard was "If you bastards want to live like pigs then go ahead." Well as long as we had a path to walk through we were fine. My mom did have this thing about calling us, "sons of bitches and bastards," when she got angry. No one took it seriously. We would all call each other names, mostly retard, moron, jerk, and queer inside the house and asshole, jerk off, dumb ass when we were outside. That's about it and that mostly came from John. He took after my mom, so when we would cry to mom and say, "Mom! John called me a retard and other words that I can't repeat." Her response would be, "What the hell did you do to him, to make him call you that?" All was good.

Everyone in the family went to Driftwood Elementary for Kindergarten. It was just a block away at the top of Claremont Street. My father and his brothers and sister went there. After Kindergarten, we all attended Holy Sacrament Catholic School for first grade through eighth grade. My mother went there. A typical morning would be Mom at the bottom of the stairs calling us.

"Jimmy, Johnny, Gerald, and, Phillip! Get up and get ready for school."

We'd get out of our bunk beds, circle the toilet, pee, wash our face and hands, put on our school pants, and run downstairs. Mostly we would eat a bowl of Kellogg's cornflakes cereal for breakfast. In winter, we would stop by the heater, sit on the floor each of us on one of the four sides and put our feet on the grating. Breakfast then was Quaker Oats hot oatmeal. My mother would iron our school dress shirts while we ran upstairs to brush our teeth. After each of us finished, we would run back downstairs to put on our shirts and our neckties. I would need a little help with this. After that, we'd put on our dress shoes that we left on the steps. We would run back in the kitchen where my mother was standing next to a glass of water and a long barber style unbreakable comb and comb our hair. She would dip the comb in the water to help hold our hair in place. Then she would tell us how handsome we were before sending us out to school. We would meet other kids coming down Cole Street and still others coming up Claremont Street. School wasn't far, a block up Claremont Street, then turn right for one block down Huddle Street, a left on Hampton Road for two blocks, across Market Street to Holy Sacrament School. The public school kids would start an hour later so we would not see them until after 4 p.m.

The Sisters of Saint Jerald's were the nuns responsible to teach in the Philadelphia Archdiocese, and that included us. The sisters were mostly cool. They wore the classic habit with the raised black veil. This was supported by white cloth with so much starch that it seemed as if it were made of cardboard, and a giant white "cardboard" bib, a long black dress and Rosary Beads dangling off their hip. They had old lady black high top shoes and black stockings and kept themselves covered, even when it was hot. They would not say the name of Jesus without bowing their head and made the sign of the cross whenever an ambulance would go by. The nuns were good teachers, but it seemed as if they learned their student control techniques from the Curly, Larry and Moe school of discipline.

The first two times I remember being slapped in the face were in the first grade by Sister Alice Vincent, One of my classmates, Michael Petka, was being punished for something. Jealousy overcame me and I wanted some of his attention. I started to laugh out loud and Sister told me to come up to the front of the class. Michael was then laughing at me. I was standing next to Michael shoulder to shoulder both facing the class. It was showtime. All in one swing, she gave us both a slap across the face. As we recovered we both started laughing at each other's stupid looks, when all of a sudden - *Whack! Whack!* Within a millisecond we were both slapped again and now facing away from each other and not laughing anymore. The next step we both knew:

"Go to opposite sides of the classroom and face the corner." If I only knew the lesson to be learned by standing in the corner, I would have been a genius by the time I was in the fourth grade.

I ended up passing on "Trial" that year. "Passing on "trial" meant that the teacher wanted you to repeat that grade but in my case, it was a close call so my mother asked them to let me try to make up for my failures in the first semester of the next grade. Passing on trial is how it went for me the next three years.

I don't know what it was with me. My parents were smart enough; all the other kids in my family were Honor Roll students. I tried and tried but nothing worked. Even the other kids in my class, like Michael, who was unruly and "bad," seemed to get passing grades. Most adults thought I was being lazy and that angered some of them.

It didn't help that I wrote with my left hand. One nun told me that she knew why I was so bad. It's because I was left-handed just like Lucifer. I wished I could understand them. I just couldn't comprehend, so most of the lessons they taught went in my ears and somehow got muffled; therefore, not making any sense to me and disappearing. Even playing sports I had trouble listening and learning. One case I remember was when I signed up for football the coach wanted me to play quarterback, so, I tried. He gave me the play to give to the team in the huddle; the play was supposed to be a Half-Back Quickie on two. I thought he said half baked cookie on two. I kind of knew that something wasn't right when the team started to express amusement. After that, the coach moved me to the defensive team.

On the home front in 1963 just after our youngest sibling, Ruth, was born and our oldest sister Elizabeth graduated from Manchester High School my father got sick. Something was wrong with dad. Mom said he came home from work and was exhausted. He was an above-average guy about 5'10" tall and 150 pounds. His brother, Uncle Phil was sickly, but Dad always seemed healthy to me. The doctors sent him to Sacred Heart Hospital in Castleton for a couple of weeks We were too young to go in to see him, so we would sit out in the car and Dad would come to the window and wave to us. That was reassuring. You see, Dad hardly ever beat us. There were times when we got the belt and we knew it was coming, but never in anger.

Dad was mostly cool, calm, and collected and he expected us to be the same. He taught us how to behave by example. His actions taught us to be like him and that it was cool to behave. Finally, after three weeks in the hospital dad was diagnosed with Tuberculoses or TB for short. At the time TB was considered highly contagious and that meant he was going to be sent away to a sanatorium in upstate Pennsylvania; a special place for TB patients called South Mountain. This turn of events also meant we no longer had dad's favorite meal of steak, mashed potatoes and Campbell's pork and beans on payday. We could still hear the whistle blow for the Sun Oil shift change but it didn't mean that Dad was coming home as it did before. Mom and my older sisters were able to go see Dad upstate, but the boys had to stay the night with Aunt Delores and Uncle Ron at their house with their three boys. My younger brother and sisters stayed with Aunt Mary down in Penn's Port.

Nothing exciting ever happened at Aunt Delores and Uncle Ron's. They lived out in Byrne Township. Byrne Township is where homes are separated by giant yards called acres. Their oldest son Ron Jr. is my age. John, Gerald, and I would go out to play with them and meet their friends. Jimmy was fourteen and usually stayed in, hanging out with Uncle Ron. Inevitably, John would end up calling one of our cousin's friends a retard or queer or something like that. John was not very big physically and Gerald and I outgrew him by age nine but he sure was wicked with his tongue. He would embarrass someone into just walking away or going home to tell their mother that some mean little kid said that she fed them shit sandwiches with pubic hair on top. At this time I had no idea what pubic hair was. But, by the way, John said it; I knew I didn't want any on my sandwich. This type of behavior from John would continue into his adulthood.

Not long after dad was away, Mom began to have financial difficulties. Early on, some of dad's friends from the neighborhood or work would come by and drop off some food and they gave us a used television to use when our old one stopped working. Good old Uncle Jack would take us out to get our haircut. In those days you needed to get your hair cut every month, so you didn't look as if you were unkempt. Once he bought each of us four boys brand new shoes. Uncle Jack was neat. He was an Army combat veteran from World War II where he served in France,

Uncle Jack would say, "Do you know how the French pronounce our last name? Web'stair." He would say it real fancy as if it pleased him just to say it that way. Like most combat veterans he wouldn't say much more about his time there. After he came back he had it made. He lived on the other side of Driftwood in one of the many row houses built after the war. He had a wife and a family of his own. He had a great job as an assembly line worker in a General Motors plant down in Delaware.

My parents did not have any vices that I could tell. Dad didn't drink, smoke, chase women, drive fast, or gamble. Mom was the same. And most of us children followed suit. They really did like each other and both considered their family a blessing. We all had good health, no one even wore glasses. They say I was baptized in the hospital and had to stay in there for a couple of weeks with pneumonia and that I was allergic to cow's milk. I don't remember any of that. My doctor recommended goat's instead of cow's milk. After a month, my mom decided I was as normal as any of her other kids so she started to give me cow's milk and I didn't have any ill effects. So she continued to feed regular milk to me and changed doctors.

As far as dad's illness was concerned, we didn't get much information, just that he wasn't coming home anytime soon. Nana Quinn was still living down the street until she fell off a chair and broke her hip. This was bad because; guess who she moved in with? That's right, us. Nana's hospital bed was moved into our dining room where mom took care of her. Nana needed a lot of care. This was the time we were all introduced to the bedpan. Now, fortunately for me, I was born in the era of the flushing toilets and therefore not to have your poop and pee immediately flushed away was a traumatic experience to me. When Nana needed her bedpan cleared, mom would call into the next room to whoever was there to take the bedpan upstairs to be emptied in the toilet. The few times when I did this, my brothers would tease me about having a pan of human excrement in my hands. The duty was always taken care of and as often as John battled with Nana he never complained about helping with her care. We just didn't like it very much. Did I mention there was nothing wrong with Nana's eating habits and that her bedpan was white enamel which showed the contrast of colors very well? We had to carry it through the living room, no way were we allowed to carry it through the kitchen. God bless Nana. What a humiliating experience that had to have been for her. Nana used to say," I never cursed until I moved in with you devilish sons-a-bitches and bastards."

My oldest sister, Elizabeth, announced she wanted to join the convent. I never asked why, but it wasn't a far-out idea considering her conservative lifestyle. Elizabeth, most of us called her Betty, told me later that dad asked her to wait a year before joining the convent. Betty agreed and spent her time working in a hoagie shop in Upper Manchester. Ann also graduated from Manchester High School around this time and started to work at a hoagie shop in Driftwood. Hoagie shops sold steak sandwiches almost always with melted cheese on top, potato chips, sodas', tasty cakes, and hoagies. Hoagies are sandwiches made from different kinds of thinly sliced Italian meat, mainly boiled ham (Capicola), Genoa salami and provolone cheese in an Italian roll. My sisters having jobs helped a little. They could at least bring home some spending money. My mom didn't drive so Elizabeth would take her up to see dad. Nana helped pay some bills when she received her social security checks. She sold the house on Claremont Street and that had to have helped, but a lot of it went to pay her hospital bills.

While dad was in the hospital we all had to go to the old Castleton hospital that was converted into a TB clinic. Our family had to go there for checkups every six weeks. Our height and weight were measured; we received an injection of medicine to make sure we were all okay. John was the only one the doctors were concerned with because of his slow physical growth rate. Eleven months later, Dad finally came home from the hospital. I remember hearing he was going to get dropped off up on

Manchester Avenue, so Mary, Joan, and I ran up to the corner to meet him. Kevin may have followed but I don't remember. When Dad got home we all had orange covered vanilla popsicles. It was a good day. John ended up being well enough to stop going to the clinic soon after Dad came home from the hospital. It is nice to have the family back together again. ✑

# Chapter 3 - Early Retirement

Sun Oil offered my father work, but not in the same department as before. He was sent to the mailroom and took a drop in pay and benefits. By then, he had already worked in the refinery for eighteen years. For some reason, he quit and I never saw him go to work again. I never asked why. I figured if my mother and my older siblings accepted it, I accepted it. He didn't seem sickly. It was around this time that my mother got a job at the hospital in Castleton Medical Center. As far as I know, she worked her way up to becoming a Licensed Practical Nurse. That same year Elizabeth joined the convent in Baltimore and became a nun. Ann got a job at the Castleton Bell Telephone Co. Ann getting that job could have been a good thing. But it wasn't. She met this guy named Louie Carletti from Franklin Street in Castleton. He used to hang out at the pool hall near the Red Arrow bus stop. He only took one look at my sister and that was it. Ann had the best-combined physical features from my mom and dad. Additionally, Ann had a natural mole on her left cheek and like my mother and other sisters she didn't need much make-up before looking her best. Ann's look and demeanor had an effect on some men that made them want to be with her and to have her all to themselves. She had guys calling and asking about her all the time. One night around eleven o'clock a guy came by the house. He was on the sidewalk below the girls' bedroom window singing "Oh Annie, O Annie" to the tune of Richie Valens' "Oh, Donna." He was obviously drunk and no threat so the girls started laughing at him. Nana yelled out the window; "Is that you Mr. Turner?" He was the father of one the kids on my baseball team. "Go home or I'll call the cops." We didn't hear from the Turners for a while after that.

No one knew that Louie Carletti already had a son by a girl he hadn't married. He was from another universe as far as we were concerned. Louie was a handsome guy who wore nice clothes, in a mobster kind of way. His hair was black and combed straight back and I never saw his hair out of place. He liked me for some reason and would give me a quarter for going to the store and getting him a pack of L&M cigarettes. He never worked, that I knew about. They say he got his money from his parent's candy store's cash register. Ann was only eighteen and not very worldly at the time. I guess my sister just fell in love with him.

In our area when a couple wanted to get married quickly without a lot of paperwork or delay, they could drive down to Elkton, Maryland. And that's exactly what they did. Ann along with her best friend, Shirley Post, accompanied by Louie and his best man, Bear all drove down to Maryland. Shortly after they eloped, Ann got pregnant. In less than a year, our family had a niece and a want-to-be mobster in the family. What the hell just happened?

The best part was, of course, our niece, Holly. I loved my niece like a sister; her name is Elizabeth Lee Carletti. Less than a year later Ann moved to Castleton to live with Louie and his family. But that was only for a few months. Shortly after the move, Ann and Holly returned and came back to live with us. I found out later from my brother John that Louie physically abused my sister and she couldn't stand living with him anymore.

My poor Mother! There she was - her husband ill and not working, her eldest daughter is in the convent, her second child back at home with a baby and her mother is lying in the dining room slowly recovering from hip surgery. My mother was a very strong lady. She would work the graveyard shift so she could be home to wake us up, comb our hair and send us off to school. I remember times when some neighbors needed medical care or injections and my mom and our neighbor, Mrs. Howard, would take care of them.

At that time I considered petitioning the Pope in Rome to canonize my mom into sainthood. I think a person needs three proven miracles accredited to them to become a saint. I could only think of two miracles. The first was around ten o'clock at night when mom and Mrs. Howard and another nurse were going to work. Mrs. Howard was driving. African Americans were demonstrating for their civil rights that night. Sometimes, in the mid-sixties, the demonstrators blocked traffic to get attention. During these days demonstrations occasionally turned into riots and property got damaged and people got hurt. When they blocked my mom's car, Mrs. Howard told us that she and the other nurse were terrified and praying for their lives while my mom got out of the car and yelled.

"You sons of bitches better get the hell out of my way. I got to go to work, so I can feed my kids."

Now, mom was a big woman and wearing her white nurse's uniform must have helped because those angry men just parted like the red sea and let her car pass. Mom was my hero.

Blacks were not a significant part of our life. Lower Manchester had a population of about two percent Black in those days. A few Blacks lived in Sun Village in a score of wood-frame houses built in the 1920s for the refinery workers and some other Blacks lived down on Green Street, near the railroad tracks. It seemed to me that the Blacks lived in areas that were off the beaten path. Like someone was trying to hide them or something. The city of Castleton was about sixty percent Black in those days. We would see the Blacks in the summer as they came by to empty our trashcans early in the morning. It seemed to me that they had their own language to let the truck driver know when to stop and start. To me, they were parading down Claremont Street following the garbage truck as if they were a calypso band trailing a circus elephant. They picked up each metal trash can and tossed it to each other in a natural rhythm. When the truck's air brakes were applied it sounded as if an elephant was snorting. As one of the men jumped up onto the truck to pull the mechanical lever to turn the trash up inside it sounded as if the big animal roared. They would leave a trail of banged up, tipped over metal trashcans in their wake. Lids were tossed to the side; some on the sidewalk, some tilted against the curb. But never any trash. They did their job and picked up the trash. To Timmy

Howard and me, it was quite a scene. After they passed, Timmy and I would mimic them by strutting down the street picking up the now empty trash cans and tossing them to each other; while pointing and grunting in our deepest voices. We had a ball.

When my dad worked at Sun Oil, one of the benefits was that we could go to their Athletic Association out in Byrne Township. We called it the AA. It had campgrounds, tennis courts, and a big indoor activity center. My favorite was the Olympic-sized swimming pool. One day as we approached the entrance, I looked across the street and saw some African American children; we usually referred to them as "colored" kids in a large, almost empty field playing on a set of swings.

"Who are they?" I asked my dad.

"They are the children of the colored workers," he answered.

A small set of swings was their AA. The Blacks were not allowed to come and swim in the pool except for when all Sun Oil workers' families attended day camp for two weeks during each summer. I could never figure this out. I remember this bothered me. So did the fact that I heard the term "niggers" inside and outside the house. Sometimes if you referred to Black people by any other name you got a sharp comment such as "What, are you afraid of them?" or "Maybe you'd like to marry one?" I am ashamed to say that I used that term myself for years with little thought. That was in the early sixties and sadly some things are very slow to change. I battle myself to refrain from thinking in terms of that word even to this day.

Father McMurphy was the Pastor of Holy Sacrament Parish. He was the top dog over all the Catholics in the Area. He also commanded respect from others in the community. He was a mature and direct person. One time, a despondent man tried to kill himself by jumping off the Congore Water Tower near the Holy Sacrament's Church and school. The tower is about one hundred and fifty feet high and most likely jumping from this height on to a paved parking lot would do the job of killing, or at least severely injuring a person. The police called the rectory for assistance. When Father McMurphy arrived he asked the man if he was a Catholic, and the man nodded his head, "Yes." Father said to the man, "If you want to go straight to hell, go ahead and jump. If you want another chance at getting into heaven, come down so we can talk." The man looked down, looked up and then slowly climbed down the tower.

Father Mc Murphy also listened to confessions. We Catholics had to give our confessions on Saturday before you could receive Holy Communion on Sunday. It was bad enough that you had to tell someone your secret failures, but the fact that he was hard of hearing in one ear made it ten times worse. I could never remember which side was his good ear so I could enter the confessional box on his good side. Most of the time I avoided him like the plague. On Saturdays, there was always a longer line for the other priest hearing confessions. It didn't help that a couple of noisy old ladies sat in the pews just outside the confessional door. Father McMurphy's duties also included handing out school report cards. I dreaded that day. The report card was set up so your behavior was on one side and your academics were on the other. He actually paid more attention to the behavior side. He was not pleased if he thought you were disrupting others from learning their lessons. Naturally, religion was a subject he was interested in.

I remember standing in front of the class receiving my report card and, after reading my grades aloud, he asked, "With grades like these how are you going to support yourself?"

This was not a rhetorical question. He actually wanted an answer. He would sit there, waiting, leaning his good ear towards me. I stood there inspecting the age spots on his balding head. Father repeated, "How do you expect to support yourself with these poor grades?"

I'd rather he just slap me in my face and get this inquisition over with. I have been slapped enough to know that after the initial sting the pain would quickly subside and I could go on about my business. But he didn't, he just sat, waiting. This is torture. Now, I'm thinking "What the hell is this asshole waiting for? He already knows how dumb I am. I can't even spell future, let alone get prepared for it."

He was serious about waiting for an answer so I thought for a while and just said," I don't know yet, Father."

He looked at me and said, "Try to do better next time." I think he thought he made his point and I returned to my seat, in shame.

After passing on "trial" in the first, second and third grades, I FAILED AND HAD TO REPEAT THE FOURTH GRADE. Miss Massey was a lay teacher and was one of three non-nuns in a school of sixteen teachers. She had a mannish look about her. She was at least six feet tall with wide shoulders and short, dark hair. Even then, I sensed she didn't like being a woman. In my more bitter times, in reference to her lack of femininity, I would say she was the only one "man" enough to fail me.

Flunking the fourth grade was very embarrassing for me. I remember not going straight home from school that day. It was the last day of school and everyone was anxious to get home so they could start their summer vacation. I just wandered around Driftwood not wanting to go home and having to disappoint my mother and father. I watched as all the other kids went home, changed from their school clothes, and come back out to play before I decided to go home and face my parents. When I finally went home I didn't get in trouble. My mom just said to me, "How could you let this happen?" I didn't have an answer.

My second year in the fourth grade I was kind of in a state of shock. I only remember two things. One, they didn't hit me anymore. I think some law passed where teachers weren't allowed to give corporal punishment anymore. I think it was written somewhere in the Second Ecumenical Council. I remember getting in trouble again and what Miss Massey said, "Corporal punishment is not allowed anymore so I want you to hit yourself. The pretzel delivery driver gave me this steel ruler for children just like you." I said to myself, there is no way this was going to happen. It was me and Dennis Carey. We just looked at each other with the look that said, you first. She gave us another threat, "I'm going to send you to Father McMurphy if you don't." That was enough for Dennis. He grabbed the ruler from her and started to strike himself across the back of his other hand. She asked if I was going to let Dennis be the only one punished for something that we both did; that being talking in class. I would love to say that I didn't follow, but as the saying goes "if he jumped off a bridge would you follow." Yep! I did. I was so mad at myself for doing that.

The other thing I remember from that school year was even worse. It was November when Mother Louise Gertrude came to our class and asked Miss Massey to go out in the hall with her. Everyone knew something was wrong because when the classroom door opened we could see other nuns gathering around weeping. Right away without knowing exactly what happened, some of the girls in my class started to cry. Mother Superior came in our room and told us that President Kennedy and his wife were visiting Dallas when some man shot and killed him. Mother Superior then asked us all to join her in saying the rosary. This was a very sad day.

In September of 1964, I started the fifth grade. I was over the shock and major embarrassment of repeating the fourth grade. But as far as school was concerned, I was generally pissed off at the whole situation. Poor Sister William Delores, she had to deal with my attitude. She was the prettiest nun I've ever seen, but still, I didn't care anymore. What could they do to me? They already hit and humiliated me in front of my classmates until I cried. They made sure everyone knew that I was late paying my book bill. After October, all the students still owing money had their names listed on the side blackboard. As a student paid his or her book bill, Sister would erase their name. It was only $16.00 per student a year but my mom just didn't have it.

At that time, there were four or five of us Websters going to Holy Sacrament and Mom was sending James and John to St. Paul, the all-boys Catholic High School. Why mom and dad didn't send the girls to St. Mary's, the local all-girls Catholic

High school, I don't know, because my mom went there. At St. Paul's, a student had to buy their own books instead of renting them as we did in grade school. Gym clothes cost money and, since St. Paul was in Castleton, they had to take a bus and have lunch money. Dad still didn't work outside the house but Ann and Holly, now separated from Louie, were living with us. Ann went to St. Joseph College in Philly and was a student teacher at age nineteen when she began to teach the fourth grade at St. Hedwig's Catholic School in Castleton. Katherine got a job at the Ship and Shore clothing distribution center and helped with the bills.

When my sisters got paid they would send us up to the store to get their favorite treat. It was always the same thing. They would say, "I want a bottle of Pepsi and a bag of Herr's potato chips and a Tasteykake." The only difference was, Ann wanted a Chocolate junior Tasteykake and Katherine wanted Butterscotch Krimpets. Well, it didn't take John long to be schooled in the art of running errands. We weren't going to the store for treats unless we got something for ourselves. We asked our sisters, "Why should I go to the store for you?" "Because I said so," was the response. We just laughed at that. Typically, if mom asked us to go we went without any questions. Of course, we would go for something essential but not for treats. When that did not work they would concede. "You can have the two cents deposit from the empty soda bottle and you can lick the icings off the Tasteykake wrapper." That was it. That was all we needed to run up the block to the newly built Howie's market and get them their treat. I can't tell you why they didn't just go themselves but they never did. After a few times, they stopped asking John because he figured out that if you rubbed the tops of the Tasteykake on the way home more icing would stick to the wrapper. I was never able to figure this trick out. I'd go to the store every time.

Katherine helped buy the family car when the old 1955 Ford station wagon broke down. We did without a car for a few months, borrowing the Howard's family Rambler before Katherine could put enough money down at a car lot.

The nuns always said that going to Catholic school was a privilege, not a right. I still didn't care. The gloves were off. I was bad, unruly, and a menace to my fellow classmates. I remember after Sister changed our seats, I did not want to sit down next to this girl because I thought she was fat and ugly, so for the first day I just stood up next to my seat. I was a jerk and a half (I'm sorry Karen Lopper.) Timmy Howard swears I was the reason he failed the fifth grade. I did do some foolish things. There was this song that was popular at the time by the English Rock and Roll group, The Kinks - "I'm so tired, tired of waiting for you." Well, when Sister would use the expression "I'm tired of waiting for you children to learn this," that was my cue. I would jump out of my seat and start singing. "So tired, tired of waiting, tired of waiting for you ou ou ou ou." I used to walk around the classroom and, just before I would turn a corner, I would tilt my head in the direction I was turning. I took advantage of Sister's kindness. I could tell she would never slap me or hurt me in any way. (Sorry Sister William Delores.) ☙

## Chapter 4 - Opening My Scope

Driftwood was divided by Market Street, separating north from south, and we lived on the south side. In a sarcastic attempt to mimic South Philadelphia, my brother Jimmy used a black magic marker to make tee shirts with "South Driftwood" writing across the front. As in, don't mess with me I'm from South Driftwood. Sun Oil Refinery covered Driftwood down to the Amtrak railroad tracks that separated us from Penn's Port. Everything north of Market St. was referred to by us as, "The other side of Driftwood." People over there called their area Driftwood Terrace. Driftwood Terrace was loaded with people. There were a lot of row homes so tightly packed together that cars could only park diagonally on one side of the street. Uncle Jack lived here and so did most of the kids that I went to school and played little league baseball with. We would all meet at the Youth Center on Market Street to play games. My favorite was dodge ball. I was good at this, too. There was a level of enjoyment in hitting certain kids just as hard as I can while inflicting little damage to them. On Saturday evenings, they would have dances where we would listen to the new Beatles songs and dance to Motown music. Songs were simple then, "She loves you, Yea Yea Yea." That was neat, a guy telling his buddy that it's not all lost because his girlfriend still loves him. And a guy just wants to hold her hand. They also ask the question; "If I fell in love with you?" And Smokey Robinson saying; "I don't want you but I need you." This was wonderful stuff.

A lot of girls liked my brother John. He was nice looking, always acted cool even when he was cutting you up with verbal comments, and he could dance. He had a dark Irish look with light skin, dark hair, and blue eyes. Gerald and I were okay at dancing, but not like John. A few of the guys from Claremont St. would be there; Simon Adams, Timmy Howard, and Bobby Britt.

Simon was John's age and our leader. Simon was well known for being an outstanding athlete. He received a college scholarship to play basketball and ended up playing professionally in Europe. The stress of being that talented must have been overwhelming because there were times when Simon played with his "doodle" in front of us. He used to try to get us to join in this activity with him but only Bobby would take the bait. This behavior was senseless to me. Because he was able to bring himself to a climax, made me wonder whether he was normal or what; I didn't know what to think. Simon danced pretty well and we all did splits while dancing to James Brown songs. Timmy was an okay dancer. Bobby couldn't dance a lick. He danced like an unoiled machine. John called him, "friction in action." While Bobby was dancing, John would tell him he looked like he needed to take a shit.

A few Blacks from Green Street would attend. I remember on one occasion this one colored guy approached me. His name was Clarence Ross and he wanted the shirt I was wearing. It was a pink button-up dress shirt with a button-down collar. I wore it casually and not tucked into my pants. He pointed to the manufacture's stamp showing on my shirttail and said it looked like a potato sack on me. He said I should take it off and give it to him. This surprised me. First, that he even asked that question the way he did. It wasn't as if I was standing by myself somewhere in a corner or was alone in the bathroom. I was out in the middle of the dance floor. I was standing within a circle of friends. Secondly, he was serious. John and Gerald saw what was going on and said, "Let's go, Phillip," and we just walked away. I also remember Timmy Howard coming up to me and saying that he accidentally bumped into one of the Rider brothers and they wanted to beat him up after the dance. Of course, this wasn't going to happen either. I told Timmy to stay close to me until the dance was over and together with John and Gerald we walked out the door.

Mostly, we had a lot of fun dancing the twist but I could never master the dance called the Bristol Stomp. Once, there were these twin Black girls who liked John and me. Their names were Mira and Maria Cotton. They were nice girls. We used to walk them home after the dances and on the way, we would stop by Romeo's Hoagie shop to get an Italian bread roll with some olive oil on it and a Pepsi Cola. After we sat and ate the hoagie rolls, the girls would cross Hampton Road and walk down Green Street by themselves. We didn't go down Green Street for two reasons - it was away from where we lived and the other reason, I couldn't figure out why, but there was an unwritten rule that Whites would stay away from the Black homes and they would stay away from ours. I don't know whatever happened to those nice girls, but a few years later Clarence Ross shot and killed a boy in Castleton and he went to prison for a long time.

Things continued the same for me in school through the sixth grade. Sometimes, when I would come in from recess, I would find a picture of a saint with a large soft pretzel and candy hidden in my desk. And when the other students had to write a 100-word composition on some subject, Sister told me to write a letter to my sister Elizabeth and she would mail it for me. (Another cool thing was the name Elizabeth picked when she took her final vows, Sister Phillip Lea.) My sixth-grade teacher, Sister Rose Benedict never said a word about the gifts of candy and stuff and neither did I. (Thank you, Sister Rose.)

When the school year ended, I had to go to summer school and I wasn't happy about it. I blamed Sister Rose because my Mom said she recommended it. That year they had a government-funded program where Catholic schoolchildren were accepted into the public school system for summer school. It was for poor and slow learning kids, like me. It was out at Morgan Elementary and a lot of guys I went to Holy Sacrament with were there and so were some other kids that dropped out of Catholic School in earlier grades. Other kids I knew from Little League baseball also attended. After a day or so, I felt comfortable. There were a few Black kids there also. We were all in it together. The teachers there were all women lay teachers. They started with the basics; I mean third-grade addition, subtraction, multiplication, and easy spelling. All the stuff I didn't get the first time around. For some reason, I couldn't grasp things as quick as most other children. Once my teachers moved on to the next level in the subject, I was still trying to make sense of the introduction and routinely became lost.

But now hearing it again, I caught on real quick. At summer school the teachers took their time because we were all slow. I think the agenda was changed from meeting a goal set to some smart person's standards to "let's teach these kids the lessons until they learn it." Soon, I started to excel in this environment and became the "smartest of the dummies." The rule here is once you learned the lesson you could go out for recess. Finally, I was smart. My father would drive me to school every day and come to pick me up when it was over. We would start at 8 a.m. and finish by noon. We got free lunches with dessert. We went to museums and plays and even got our teeth fixed. I'm actually glad I went. Even the dentist part, though it hurt. I thank them because I still have all my teeth today.

My mom had the spirit to motivate herself and the soul to stay deeply committed, but still, her struggles continued. I don't know whose idea it was, but Dad decided to go to Florida. I know that Mom used to live down there with her aunt and that we would vacation in Fort Lauderdale when Dad was still working. But, to just get up and go and try to move down there did not seem as if it was a good idea to me. When Dad went, he drove the car and took Ann, her daughter Holly, Katherine and James. James was still in High School. He and John stopped going to St. Paul High School earlier that year. It was the beginning of John's freshman year. I was told that someone broke into Jimmy's gym locker and stole his gym clothes. The very next week someone broke into John's locker and stole all of his schoolbooks. Since we couldn't afford to replace them they both had to leave. So my two oldest brothers went to Manchester High School. I felt bad for Jimmy because he was doing well at St. Paul. He was on the cross-country track team and received a medal for doing well in chemistry. Without asking for my opinion, off went my dad and my older siblings.

John was now the man of the house. Gerald was next than me, with Mary, Joan, Kevin and Ruth still at home. God help us one and all.

Mom continued to work as a nurse at the hospital and Nana remained living with us. The whole time dad didn't work we never went on welfare or received any kind of public assistance, except if you count the TB shots we got at the clinic and the summer school I went to in 1965. My parents were not going to allow it. My mom always said that we were independently wealthy because we were independent of the love of money and material things. We did without and we made ends meet. We were frugal before I realized there was a word for it. It helped that we were easily contented. And that is a lesson well learned. My mom would get paid every other Thursday. The second Monday, Tuesday and Wednesday were always the toughest. There were times when we would run low of food and heating oil and have to turn on the stove for heat and have dry cereal for breakfast, tea, crackers and peanut butter for lunch, and grilled cheese sandwiches for dinner. Nana would order some raisin bread, milk and butter to be delivered to the house throughout the month and she could wait to pay for it at the end of the month when she got her social security check. She always said at least you kids had some bread to put in your bellies before you went to school in the morning.

We didn't hear much from Florida, except that Jimmy was enrolled at Fort Lauderdale High School. He used my mom's friend, Janie's home address while they lived in a motel. Ann got a job at a restaurant and was receiving plenty of tips. Holly stayed with Janie while Ann worked. Katherine got a job selling tickets at a horse racetrack and my dad started to work cutting grass at a golf course. After a month they moved from a motel and into their own two-bedroom duplex.

It was time for mom's second miracle. We were all getting hungry; it was ten days since mom's last paycheck. It was cold that winter in Pennsylvania and the previous payday she chose to pay for gas, electric, and heating oil first and whatever was leftover for food. It was Sunday and we didn't have any money and barely any food left in the house. There was no money in the bank, so Mom couldn't write a personal check. Even if there wasn't any money to cover the amount of the check, sometimes on Wednesdays after five in the evening she wrote checks for food. And then, after working the night shift she would stay up Thursday morning and deposit part of her paycheck to cover the check she wrote the night before. It's not as if you could lift the sofa cushions or dig down in the sides and find money, we already cut out the bottom piece of cloth a while ago. If a guest ever dropped money out of their pocket all you had to do was lift up the cushioning to see what little prize was in there. And then shake the couch and pick up the loose change. Those days it was only cracker crumbs, bobby pins, and assorted marbles. We didn't drink soda so there weren't any 2 cents per bottle deposit. All these things were used up by the second Monday after mom's payday. None of us would let anyone outside the family know we were that desperate. When we went outside, we pretended like everything was honky dory. We all searched the house and neighborhood and came up with fifty-eight cents. Mom sent John and Gerald to the Acme Market and they came home with a box of spaghetti, a box of corn flakes, powder milk and three packs of Kool-Aid. For three days and nights, nine people ate plenty and filled our bellies. To me, that was miracle number two.

Soon after that, Mom developed blood clots in her legs and was hospitalized. This was not good. I was 12 years old then, Gerald was 13 and John was 14 years old. We were not what they called "Irish Twins," but we were close. Our birthdays were fourteen months apart. Nana was now the only adult in the house. She was able to get around with a cane but didn't go out of the house very much. Nana's relatives hardly made contact with her. Her brother, James the Priest, was in a parish in upstate Pennsylvania. Her brother, John the Army Brigadier General, would send a card from Europe or someplace he was visiting, and her brother Joe, from Wilmington, Delaware, well, he never came around. At least, he didn't come around, not any time that I know of, I guess it was not a good business decision to visit your poor relatives. Nana didn't handle the pressure of being poor and having us kids around very well. She and John battled a lot. They would end up in a verbal battle trying to curse each other out. John won every time. He had a lot more experience with foul language. Mom was stuck in the hospital hoping the clots didn't move up her leg. Nana gave John, Gerald, and me each two quarters and said, "Take the bus up to see your mother," and we did. It was weird seeing mom there and not home with us. By time payday passed, we were hurting. We weren't starving but we were hungry and we didn't know where our next meal was coming from. As days passed, and without any money coming in, we ran out of heating oil. In the past, we usually turned on the oven and opened the stove burners, but this time we didn't pay last month's utility bill and the utility companies were about to turn off the gas and electric. Nana panicked and called for state relief. My mom told me later that a representative from the Department of Public Welfare came to her hospital bed and told her that if she did not sign to accept the help the state offered, they would consider her unable to support her children and, that dad abandoned his kids, and the state would take custody. She conceded to the pressure and signed up for relief. We began to receive large rectangle blocks of cheese, big tubs of peanut butter, and several loaves of day-old bread. When my mom came home from the hospital, she was very angry with her Mother. Nana said that she couldn't stand by and let the kids starve. I didn't know why mom was so angry. It probably had to do with a story mom told me years later. She said, "Just after giving birth to Kevin, her tenth child, a doctor admonished her for having so many kids. That tongue-lashing affected her into becoming determined to support all of her children no matter what her circumstances were. Personally, I would accept the help if I was in that situation.

Soon after my mom was released from the hospital she returned to work. Two weeks later we were off relief. Even after my mom went back to work, there were tough times. Some of the neighbors helped a little by calling up to the house and asking if one of the kids would run up to the store for them. One lady, Mrs. Wynn, would give us ten cents for going to get the afternoon paper for her. Once, one of my grandmother's friends baked a cake and sent it over. This was a treat. On Saturday morning, as soon as it opened, we would go up to the Acme market on Manchester Avenue. We helped the ladies bring home their groceries. In those days most everybody walked to the Market and the ladies pushed the shopping carts home. To save them a trip back to the store, we would push the cart for them and help them bring the groceries into their kitchen and return the cart for them for a tip. Some were generous and would give a quarter instead of a nickel and a dime. I was never aggressive enough. I was too shy to step ahead of someone to get the generous tippers. Even though we would sit in a line near the cash registers, some women would just look past the first kids to ask her favorite boy to push her cart. He would move ahead of us and get the job. I don't know how they did it, but those ladies picked certain guys every time. I knew they weren't related or anything like that. They didn't push the cart any better than me. I wasn't anyone's favorite but I got my share of nice ones. Another way we made money was to cut neighbors' grass and in the winter we would shovel the snow off people's sidewalks. Gerald had a paper route but had to quit when he broke his shoulder. After my brother's injury, I took over his paper delivery duties. We all tried to do something so we didn't have to bother mom for spending money.

A month after Mom returned home from the hospital, Dad and my elder siblings came back from Florida. My sister Ann told me that dad would be so weary after working at the golf course, Katherine and she would have to help him out of the car and into their apartment. He ended up losing his job because he was not able to perform his duties as expected. On their return, they picked up a sack of oranges and a coconut with some stupid stuff carved on it and a now dark-skinned, blond-haired Holly.

Things began to get a lot better in the following months when Ann and Katherine found employment. My father was still out of work. ❧

## Chapter 5 - New Neighbors

The next school year, James attended Manchester Senior High School for his senior year along with John, as a sophomore. Gerald was going to Manchester Junior High. I was in the seventh grade and still doing the same crap as I always did. Mary, Joan, and Kevin were following close behind me at Holy Sacrament School.

It was just an average day in 1966 when James came home from the playground behind Driftwood School and told Mom, "There's a new family that moved in next door to the Simmons on Hampton Boulevard. Their name is Volpe and they used to live in the east end of Castleton. Bennie MacVee and Donnie Britt's mom said they were not allowed to play with them." Mom being the type to give everybody a fair chance told Jimmy that if he wanted to, he was allowed to be friends with them.

Their family was large mostly boys and a few girls. Besides us, there were a few families with more than ten children. I don't think it was a coincidence that we were all Catholic. The new family lived on our side of Driftwood so, when they came out to play, they used the same playground as we did.

We Websters mirrored them in ages. Their oldest son Anthony was married and lived in the west end of Castleton with his wife and five kids. The rest still lived at home. They lived in a semi-detached house converted from a three-story apartment. Salvador was the oldest, still living at home, then Matthew, Fredrico, Fiore (they called him Popeye), Samuel, and the first girl, Marie, followed by Carlo, Angelo, Silvia, Joey, Olivia, and the baby, Monica. Most of the older boys looked alike to us. They looked as if they were the Everly Brothers on steroids. all combing their wavy dark hair back and pumped up in the pompadour style. All except for Popeye, he had flat black hair parted on the side with bulging eyes and a mustache similar to Adolf Hitler.

These guys were about as tough as they come. In the late fifties, they grew up in the William Penn projects until the older boys were teenagers and the family moved up to Edgemont Avenue in east Castleton. In the mid-sixties, the nearby Interstate highway expanded and their family was forced to move out. Their old man had dark eyes that had constant black circles under them. And he walked around clinching his fist like he was going to punch someone. His legs had a slight bow and that caused him to walk like a gorilla. He always wore tan work pants and a pocket t-shirt. His brother, Sammy (Sammy "V"), was known for being one of the toughest guys outside of Philadelphia. My sister Ann knew of them because Sammy "V" was a buddy to her husband, Louie Carletti. We didn't come across them very often at first because they continued to hang around with their Castleton friends, but they did start to go to Manchester High School. Marie and her younger brothers and sisters finished the school year where they started at St. Helena Catholic School in Castleton. The two things I remember about their mother were that she seemed small and round and someone said she was only 36 years old.

I was thirteen years old and didn't have any business hanging around with them. Samuel was my age but he was street-wise and we were years apart in physical maturation. When I went to school or church at Holy Sacrament, I would walk past the front of their house. And when I cut through the playground, going to the other side of Driftwood, I could see their backyard.

I remember the first time I saw the female version of the boys. It was twelve-year-old Marie, with her three little sisters following her across the playground. I was attracted to her long black hair, hanging down in a completely natural way. She had an untamed look about her that needed my closer attention. She was surely too much for me to handle, but I needed to find out for myself.

The next Saturday some of us were playing "speedball" in front of Driftwood School. Speedball is baseball in a confined area. A pitcher stands about fifteen feet away and throws a solid rubber ball against a wall and tries to hit a rectangle strike zone marked on the wall. A batter tries to hit the ball with a bat before the ball hits the strike zone. In the middle of playing our game, Marie came around the corner of the school with some of her younger brothers and sisters. She told me later that she was not allowed out of the house unless she was watching them. One of the guys playing ball with us was Leon Craw from Huddle Street. He had met Marie before and called her over.

Leon was a ladies' man. That is if you can be one at age 13. I know I certainly was not. I was slow in reaching puberty and was shy around girls. I would not tell anyone what girl I liked in fear they would tell her. Leon was at bat when she came. He stopped the game and walked over to her with the bat in his hand. I wanted to continue playing so I tried to take the bat from him. He refused and we started to fight. In our town, if you get into a fight and people were around, they would let it continue till one or the other had a clear advantage and then they would break it up. I was able to wrestle him to the ground and gain the advantage so our teammates stopped the fight. Our fight did not seem to bother Marie or her sisters because one of her sisters said. "Why did they stop them, they should let them fight." Leon went home and I went to pick up the bat lying at Marie's feet. Simultaneously, she and I bent down to pick up the bat. That's when it happened, I saw these brown eyes that asked the question, "Who the hell are you?" At the same time, there was this sweet pungent aroma. It was a mixture of Tide laundry detergent, Prell shampoo, and her natural scent that made me drop the bat. Suddenly, one of her older brothers came and said: "Mommy wants yous to come home, right now!" And she was gone.

A few days later, I was walking home from the Post Office when Marie and my paths crossed again. This time, she was cutting through the parking lot between Driftwood School and the Post Office. She was walking back home from Howie's Market with her little sisters. The girls seemed happy since they each had a bag of penny candy. All of a sudden out comes a barrage of profanity from the littlest one, a six-year-old cutie pie, named Monica. Olivia had taken a piece of her candy. You would think she ripped a finger off in the process.

"You fucking dog, you. I hope you die in your sleep, you dirty bitch you."

Olivia just smiled and said, "Shut up or I'll take it all, you little piece of shit, you."

Silvia said," I'm telling Mommy," and, all three sisters ran ahead. You could see their back yard from where we were standing, so Marie let them go.

I said, "Is everything all right?"

She said, "It will be ok. Let them run it off."

She asked, "You're a Webster, aren't you? I didn't answer.

Which one are you, Phillip? I said, yes

So, you must be the one I saw fight with Leon the other day?

She asked in a playful way, "Do you like to fight?"

As she said this she stepped towards me. We were about the same size, but she was way ahead of me in physical maturity. I didn't answer when she started to push me.

She teased me by saying, "Would you like to fight me? Show me how you fight?"

"What, are you afraid to fight a girl?" She backed me against a grassy bank separating the schoolyard with the lower level parking lot. I tripped and fell and she jumped on top of me sitting on my stomach and pinning my arms down with her hands. She was now hovering over me with her long black hair creating a shroud of intimacy. This made me uncomfortable. That same smell that enticed me before was starting to give me this funny sensation in my stomach and between my legs. So I thrust upwards with my hips and she went flying off, this allowed me to quickly stand up and the first thing I did was to see if anyone was watching us. No one was around and her sisters were still in sight, I guess they wanted to finish their candy before they made it to their backyard.

We sat next to each other on the bank catching our breath. It seemed that she liked me and that made me want to kiss her, but I was too shy. I was afraid if I closed my eyes too soon I would miss her lips and if I kept my eyes open she would be looking right at me and my eyes would cross. I could tell she wanted me to kiss her but she wasn't going to start first. Twenty seconds seemed like an hour when I finally got the nerve to do it, and we did. I kissed her for about two seconds. The first second was a warm and soft feeling I never felt before. During the next second, the sensations felt a lot better and it continued the longer we kissed. It seemed like I was finally in the moment and I didn't need to fantasize about anything. When suddenly that feeling of when something seems too good to be true, it probably is, came over me. I stopped and looked up to see if anyone was around. When I looked towards her house I saw her mother coming straight for us. Marie saw this too and ran to meet her. As her mother came within reach she grabbed Marie by the hair and led her all the way back home, hollering at her and calling her names. I was embarrassed for Marie and I hardly even knew her. I felt that if her mother was going to act like that, I would not bother with Marie anymore. ❧

## Chapter 6 - Hanging On the Other Side

In 1967 things in our house were about the same. Nana was still living with us and now able to climb the stairs with the help of a cane. She moved into the girl's room. Nana would always eat last and then wash the dishes before going to bed for the night. Mom still worked at the hospital and by this time had developed bleeding ulcers in her stomach. She would wake up around 10:00 p.m. to go to work. On school nights I would already be in bed and Mom would go straight to the bathroom to throw up, and then wash up, and get dressed. She would put on her wristwatch and red lipstick and Jean Nate perfume on her wrist and go to work. The boy's bedroom was next to the bathroom and my bed was against the wall that divided the two rooms. I would cover my ears with my pillow trying not to hear her as she vomited. That is a very distinct and unpleasant sound. You do not have to hear it clearly to know what is going on. I never cried about this, but I should have.

The outside world was changing, but we stayed the same. After all, we were Republicans. Mom, on a good day, would walk around the house singing show tunes. As one of the kids came in she would sing, "O, Hello Dolly! It's so nice to have you back where you belong!" When someone stayed out too long she would sing, "Won't you come home Bill Bailey, won't you come home?"

My sister, Betty, was entrenched in her new vocation as Sister Phillip Lea, teaching school and every couple of years change schools around the Baltimore Archdiocese. Ann changed professions and became a nurse and worked at the same hospital as mom. She had a new boyfriend, Peter Dusseldorf, aka "El Dorado Pete" She told me that he got this nickname because he drove his own Cadillac since the age of eighteen and never worked a day in his life. He made money the old-fashioned mob way - he loaned money and gambled. Nana would bring out the Irish in herself and make up poems about people. She didn't like Ann's new boyfriend, so Nana would say in a lyrical kind of way, "Petie you might drive a big car but, it doesn't change what you are. Let yourself be gone, before the next dawn."

Katherine got a job as a Ward Clerk at a hospital in Delaware. She didn't have a boyfriend at that time. She certainly could have, she looked as if she could be Natalie Wood's sister. Jimmy graduated from Man High in June and in September joined the Air Force. John was in eleventh grade and Gerald was a sophomore. I was in the eighth grade at Holy Sacrament with Mary, Joan Kevin, and Ruth all closing in on me. Holly followed suit as if she were a Webster.

We all got along nicely and mostly didn't fight amongst ourselves. Though, sometimes Gerald and I would fight each other. Gerald was a lot stronger than I was, but I was much more coordinated. When we got into fights with other people outside neither of us lost very often. I had the advantage because, if anyone started trouble with me and Gerald was around, he would take care of them for me. Gerald didn't have the same luxury. John would say something but that's about it. James pretty much stayed out of it.

Our neighbor Timmy Howard's family was very Catholic. They lived in their grandmother's house and she had all kinds of relics and holy pictures around and no one was allowed to say any curse words anywhere near their house or yard. Timmy also had two uncles who were priests. They taught at Villanova University. In Catholic schools, certain months were called holy months. For instance, November is Holy Souls in Purgatory month. Every morning during these months, students were required to attend Mass before school started. Tim went to the altar to receive Holy Communion one morning and the priest refused to give him the communion wafer in spite of Tim kneeling with his eyes closed, hands clasped together as if he was praying and his tongue sticking out. Timmy found out later that the priest said his hair was too long and dirty and that he was not going to give a child with long dirty hair the Body of Christ. At that time, Tim looked like a young version of the lead singer Bono of the Irish rock band U2. The next day in spite of his family's connection to the church, Tim was enrolled in Man Jr. High. Our Catholic school went to the eighth grade but the elementary public schools stopped in the sixth grade. Junior high was grades seven, eight, and nine, while Senior high was grades ten, eleven, and twelve. At this time, Tim started to hang around with some guys from the other side of Driftwood and so did I. We knew them from around town. Petie Pillsbury went to Holy Sacrament and then transferred to Man High the same year Timmy did. We all got along with each other. There was Petie's cousin, Jimmie, Dave Rose, and the De'Marco brothers, Danny, and Carmine. Danny and Carmine were fraternal twins. We all had a lot in common. Me, Petie, Tim, and Jimmy were good at athletics. Danny, Dave, and Carmine joined us in a sport just to fill out a team. Except for me, they all came from average size families. Dave and I were a year older than Petie, Tim, and Jimmy, and they were a year older than Carmine and Danny. All of us repeated at least one grade in school; like minds seem to gravitate. Carmine was a "Fonzie" before there was a television show called Happy Days. Dave, Jimmy, Petie, and I were tall and thin. Tim and Danny were average and Carmine was short and pudgy. And we all had average to good looks; that is if you think Bono, with no talent, has good looks.

The Youth Center dances stopped because the morning after a dance the police found a hypodermic needle lying on the ground behind the building. We stopped going a few months before this because they changed the type of music from Motown/Rock and Roll to early acid rock. Someone from the township thought it was a good idea to change the theme from dance music to Acid Rock instead of letting us teenagers get our energy out on the dance floor; teens went there to watch strobe lights and space out.

When I was thirteen I decided to try out for a teenage baseball team in Upper Manchester called the Spartans. My neighbor, Larry Fusco, was already playing for them and he asked me to try out. I did and was happy I made the team. The coach at that time was the cousin of Danny Murtaugh, the manager of the Major League Pittsburgh Pirates. We wore black and gray uniforms just like the Major league team. Our uniforms were made of heavy cotton sleeveless grey jerseys with black t-shirts underneath. I was happy with this since my favorite player was Roberto Clemente. He played as if he never met a coach in his life, just like me. I was still the only member of my family playing organized sports and it was fine with my parents. I could walk to the ball field and it didn't cost much money to sign up. You needed talent because if you weren't good enough you didn't make it past try-outs. Other than that, all you needed was a glove and spiked shoes. Everybody else except me had spiked shoes so Larry Fusco gave me a pair of his used ones. I still had my six-fingered baseball glove from when I was eleven years old. Before then I used any old glove I could get. I didn't want much, but when I was in little league I wanted a six-fingered baseball glove. The web between the thumb and index finger was patterned in the shape of a finger, hence a six-fingered baseball glove. I remember asking my dad if I could get one. He said, "What are you going to do with the sixth finger stick your "doddle" in it?" The Webster's' family called what a boy had a doddle and the girls had a "La La." That comment was about as racy a comment I'd ever heard coming from my father. The next Christmas I got my new six-fingered baseball glove.

We were a very private family when it came to sex. No one ever made any comment about sex to anyone else in the family. Calling someone a queer just didn't register. A "queer" or a "fairy" was a boy who acted as if he were a girl. That's all there was to it, a "sissy" was the same thing. It seemed to me that everyone used name calling to get people to change. Even when I was in grade school playing at recess when my shirttail came out of my pants the nuns called me "Mary." I guess she was referring to my shirt looking as if it were a girl's skirt when not tucked into my pants. At the time, I didn't understand what they were talking about so I simply ignored them. That's another advantage about playing an athletic game; it takes my mind off of other things.

Only a few of us had a steady boyfriend or girlfriend. Elizabeth symbolically married Jesus and Ann married Satan's understudy, Louie.

If Katherine did anything, she kept it a secret. James did the same. John had Alice Carr; they were both very small for their age and became friends in the first grade. Catholic schools had a thing for lining boys and girls side by side according to their height. Even though Alice went to a different high school, she and John continued their friendship through the years. Gerald had a couple of steady girlfriends throughout the years and most of the time they were pretty girls. I didn't have a girlfriend, yet.

In 1968 I was fourteen and in the eighth grade and there was a lot of chaos happening all around the country. There wasn't a damn thing I could do about any of it. They killed Dr. Martin Luther King Jr., and a couple of months later the same thing happened to Senator Robert F. Kennedy. Some of the guys from Cole and Claremont Streets joined the Army and went to Vietnam. Joey Jackson, Johnny James, and Paul Walklett all served in Vietnam. Jimmy was in the Air Force and got lucky and was stationed in South Korea. It seemed as if every time I watched television, something bad was happening. There was a body count on the evening news. They would list how many South Vietnam army soldiers were killed, missing, or wounded. They would list how many North Vietnam army soldiers and Viet Cong killed, or captured. They would list the US causalities by each branch of the services. They kept score as if it was a fucking game or something. The news broadcast would show protesters from all over the US and the world. It seemed to me, seeing the world as a whole; our war was just a sideshow. The Irish Catholics and Protestants fought each other, the Jews and their Arab neighbors. Africans were fighting the White colonialists for independence. It was a very sad and volatile time.

Mom continued to work at the hospital and we all did our best to stay out of trouble so as not to give her any more grief. My final year playing for Holy Sacrament basketball went well. We played on Saturdays and my mom and dad came to a couple of our games. That made me feel as if I could give mom and dad something to cheer about and it made me feel satisfied. ∾

# Chapter 7: Public School

In September of 1968, I was turning fifteen and about to start the ninth grade at Manchester Junior High School. Most of us called our local junior and senior high schools "Man" Junior High or "Man" Senior High. Sadly, someone tried to burn the junior high school down the previous summer, but the arsonist only succeeded in destroying half of the structure. Because of the lost classrooms, the School Board decided to divide all of the junior high students into two groups; one group in the morning session and the other into afternoon. Man Junior High had a rating system that assigned each student in a classroom with students of like learning abilities. Section 9-1 was for smart kids and so on until the lowest section 9-12; for the not so smart ones. I was put into 9-11. Whoopi! I was one step above the Neanderthals; a freshman Cro-Magnon. The entire ninth grade and the first six sections of eighth-graders went to classes in the morning and the lower six sections of eighth-graders and all of the seventh graders attended the afternoon session. All the guys I was hanging around with were in the lower groups of the eighth grade so they went to the afternoon session. This also included three of the Volpes; Popeye, Samuel, and Marie

I was excited about going to a public school where subjects were easier and we had different teachers for each subject and was really excited when I got all C's on my first semester report card. It was an enormous relief when I found out they just handed you the report card and asked you to have it signed by a parent and returned. This is unlike my Catholic School where the parish priest read your grades aloud in front of the class before handing you your report card. Not one D; if only Father Mc Murphy could see me now.

All C's worked out for me because at Man High if you were failing any subject you couldn't play sports, and I wanted to play basketball for Manchester Junior High. Previously, when I was in the 6th, 7th and 8th grades I was the starting point guard for our Catholic School and we did very well. Point guard is the player that brings the ball up the court to start the offensive plays. I was sure that I could make this school's starting lineup. All who signed up needed to report to the boy's locker room for a physical examination. When we got there, we were told to take off everything except our underpants. I never had to do this before when joining a team, so if I could just get past this without someone seeing my gentiles exposed I would have it made. That would be embarrassing because unlike most of the other boys, I hadn't reached puberty. I was next in line and it seemed a breeze. Everybody was going up sticking out their tongue so the doctor could give it a look, get their blood pressure taken. I cleaned my ears because I knew the doctor was going to look into them as well. I was as ready as I could be; I even put on clean underwear.

Then, while facing the doctor and everyone else standing in single file behind you, the doctor asked you to pull down my underpants so he could put his fingers in your groin area, asked you to turn your head to the left and cough, then turn to the right and cough. Just like that, it was over. When it became my turn I stepped up to the doctor and he said turn around so I can look at your back. It must have been the way I was standing in line because he ran his finger down my spine and said you have curvature of the spine. He wrote something on my medical card and said, "You can't play sports for this school." I was embarrassed and surprised. I never had any problems with my back before. I went home and didn't say a word to anyone about what the doctor said.

Three weeks later my mom asked why I wasn't playing basketball. When I told her she was upset because she knew that my back was fine so she took me to our family doctor. After examining me, he said I was fine and I just had a slight curve and it would be all right with proper posture. His remedy was for me to start carrying my schoolbooks on the other side of my body. I was thinking; well, he better think of something else because I never carried any books on either side of my body. I just said okay. He gave me a note to say I would be okay to play sports for the school. The next day I showed the school-nurse the note and a few days later they allowed me to join the team.

The starting five had already been selected. One of the starting guards was a guy that played on my little league baseball team. He was a good athlete, but he didn't make the All Star Team, as I had. No hard feelings, but his nickname was "Shorty." Imagine being beat out on a basketball team by some White kid named Shorty. I stayed on the team anyway getting some "scrub time" as we used to call it. I was tempted to show up the starters on my team by defending them during practices but the coach told me to back off and that he was running the practice.

My ninth-grade class had a dance in the school's gym and I invited Marie to go with me. I was taking a chance to ask her. Her father was very strict and for some reason, he hated me. I never met the man in my life, yet he hated me. And if he hated me, all of his boys hated me. They had no earthly reason for their hatred. The fact that they disliked me so much didn't bother me and, they didn't scare me either. The way I saw the situation was that my family was as large as theirs and we lived in Driftwood first. Elizabeth was older than their oldest brother Anthony. Besides that, I thought we were smarter than they were. Also, we had Mom on our side. I always had a feeling that a protective blanket was covering me.

Even though Marie and I drifted apart since our first kiss, I still liked her. In spite of the fact that her parents almost never let her out with a boy, she said yes to going to the dance with me. On the evening of the dance she came over to my house with two of her cousins and my dad drove us all to the dance. We had a good time. When I said goodnight to Marie, I couldn't find the right moment to give her a kiss. So we didn't even kiss each other goodnight. After that night, we drifted apart again. I think it was because she was still more physically and emotionally more mature than I.

The next spring I played baseball with the Spartans for a second season and had a good year. On one occasion my name was in the local paper for making a good catch. It must have looked like I did it on purpose but what really happened was that the spikes Larry gave me the year before were getting tighter as my feet started to grow. While playing left field, I was running in for a sinking line drive in a critical point of the game. I stumbled forward reached out catching the ball just before it hit me in the face. I tumbled over and showed the umpire the ball before I threw the runner out for leaving second base too early. This caused a double play which ended the game. As a result of the play, we won by one run.

Township officials started to have dances at the Driftwood firehouse on Friday nights. Timmy, Petie, Jimmy, Danny, Carmine, and I started to attend these dances. We had a lot of fun. There were a lot of girls and a lot of good music to watch the girls dance to. Around this time, another guy moved into Driftwood terrace from Queens Village in the West End of Castleton. His parents sent him to live with his cousins, who lived next door to Danny and Carmine DeMarco. His name was Gunther Price and he started to hang around with us. He was my age and we got along pretty well. He must have been really good looking because all the girls wanted to meet him. He liked to laugh at stupid stuff, play ball, and hang out just like we did.

Petie, Tim, Danny, Gunther, and I were hanging out as we always did. We were outside a local girl's house one night. She was home alone and wanted some company. She knew all of us and invited us in. Things got boring, so Tim went upstairs to have a bowel movement. Not to my surprise, he decided to do it in her father's bedroom slippers that were lying adrift on the bathroom floor. He called me up to watch and guard the bathroom door. The other guys knew something was up because they could hear me laughing at the sight of Timmy squatting and grunting over the home owner's slippers. Petie and Danny started to make a scene and began to call us queers, so I opened the door just enough to let them see what Tim was doing and that caused them to start laughing and pushing harder to get in. This seemed to relax Tim because he did the deed. He left without even covering it up, so I threw a towel over it and left. With all the noise we were making, I was sure the girl would find out what we were doing. As it turned out, she was preoccupied at the time. To my surprise, Gunther was in her bedroom having sex with her. I had no idea that something like that might happen. I didn't know girls my age did that stuff. Aren't you supposed to go steady first?

That crazy conflict was still going on in Southeast Asia. More and more guys from Driftwood were going over to serve as combatants. Tommy Aaron was one Marine who wasn't coming back. They said the small river craft he was in was hit by a rocket and he was killed. We all knew the Aarons. I played Teener and Little League baseball with his brother, Ron. And his brother Mickey used to hang with Danny DeMarco.

Marie's brother Matthew was a Radio Repairman in Vietnam. Matthew saw a lot of action during his tour of duty. Marie told me that he received two purple hearts for the wounds he suffered. He didn't talk about his time over there. A couple of years later I saw a scar on his arm and asked him how he got it. He told me that a rocket exploded near him and metal fragments caused the scars.

I was sixteen years old and a sophomore in high school that May in 1970. I liked this girl who was in the eighth grade. She was only fourteen but cute, clean, and a little shy. Her name was Sally Cohen. We meet at the dance where we would get together for slow dances and at 11 p.m. when the dance ended, I'd walk her home. She was well developed for her age and, because of this, she was made fun of by other girls. I felt a little sorry for her and knew that a lot of guys would take advantage of her youthful mind to get a chance at her maturing body. I had no such intentions. She was an only child to a single mother. I dated this girl for about six months but never met her mother. She lived right in the middle of Driftwood Terrace. The area was crowded but tranquil. We would take our time walking and talking as we strolled to her house. Because she didn't seem to have a curfew, we would usually just sit on her front step, talk, and have a goodnight kiss before she went inside.

One night Jane Brown stopped by. Jane was a "skank" from Upper Manchester. A "skank" is a girl who goes out with guys to have sex with them. They can be detected by the scabs on their lower legs. This is how my older brother Jimmy explained it—Shanks are girls that hang out at night, standing around smoking cigarettes, cursing, nagging and complaining about something unimportant and waiting for the right guy to hit on her. Meanwhile, mosquitoes bite her bare legs and she scratches them causing them to bleed producing scabs on her lower legs. A normal girl would know when to go home, but not a purpose-driven skank. My brother John was there while Jimmy was telling me this and added, "That's right and if she has suck marks on her neck be sure to wear a rubber"

A lot of us guys knew Jane, I knew her from one of my high school classes. As guys, a lot of time while hanging out we would talk about girls or any female not related to us and finish by saying; "Would you fuck her?" Not with a bag or two bags, just a simple, "Would you fuck her?" As in; "Did you see what Martha Wasalowski was wearing today?" Answer, "Yes." Next question, "Would you fuck her?" Well, the females would be rated by what percentage of those polled would fuck her. Jane was rated as a "thirty-seventy girl," this meaning that only three out of ten guys polled would fuck her.

Jane asked if I've seen a local guy, Bobby Truitt that night. I said, "No."

She said, "That jerk said he was going to "do it" with me tonight."

She continued to say, "All you guys are alike. You talk proud but you don't come through."

I said, "No, we're not."

She said, "Ok then, me and you down at the playground next Friday night."

After saying that, she just walked away. I was embarrassed for Sally. I told her that Jane was going to be disappointed next week too.

My girlfriend just turned to me and said, "Do you want to practice on me?"

I was surprised and a little disappointed by her cavalier attitude towards sex and just said, "No thank you." I kissed her goodnight and went home. ϵ϶

## Chapter 8: Don't Go There

In August 1970, the world continued to turn on its unbalanced axis. I was sixteen-years-old on a hot summer night when Dave, Timmy, and I decided to go to the basketball courts behind the Youth Center. There we started a 3-on-3 pickup game of basketball with some guys from Upper Man. This was a night I regretted because, usually being the unofficial leader of our group, I was able to keep everyone out of trouble. On this night, Billy Ross and Butchy Leone, a couple of older trouble makers from Driftwood, came by the courts and Billy said, "Hey all you guys, come with us, we're going up to the West End to take care of business. Butchy added, "Some guys jumped Guido and we are all going up there to kick some ass." We all knew Guido as one of the Volpe's cousins.

Well, I didn't give a shit what they wanted because I knew the Volpes' cousin, Guido, and he most likely deserved to get beat up. Plus, people got jumped every now and then. It usually started by someone asking you, "What's your name," followed by "Where you from." Once I saw these same two guys, Billy and Butchy, beat up a guy from another township just because he came to our dance and walked a girl from Driftwood home. They did this even though no one in our neighborhood was going out with her at the time; they still took it upon themselves to punish this poor guy. That night or any other night I had no interest in going to Castleton to take revenge for useless Guido. So I continued playing and tried to finish my basketball game. I did not realize until after they were gone but, my other friends, Jimmy, Petie, Carmine, and Danny went with them. None of them should have gone because we were not street fighters. We all could hold our own in a fight if needed, but we certainly did not belong in this kind of brawl.

Things changed later when Gunther showed up and said to me, "I heard that the Castleton guys knew our guys were coming and they were waiting for them." He was worried about Carmine and Danny since he was now living in the DeMarco's house for the summer. Jimmy's older brother, Alex, came over to us next and asked if I knew where Jimmy went. I told him that he went to Castleton to look for a fight and who he went with. Alex was a very straight individual and came to a panic when he heard his little brother was in what became a gang fight in Castleton. Alex asked if I would help him get his brother back. In the name of loyalty and friendship, I decided to go with Alex and Gunther to retrieve our wayward mates. The three of us walked out to the front of the Youth Center to catch a ride and that is where we met some guys getting in a car to go up to the fight. We got in the back seat. Entering from the passenger side, Alex got in first, then Gunther, and me. I told Timmy and Dave to go home and they did. Unfortunately, in the front seat were Sammy and Matthew Volpe. The driver was a friend of theirs from the East End of Castleton. At the time, Mathew was home on leave from the Army. I should have known better, especially since I did not know the driver and it didn't help that their friend was driving a black 1959 Oldsmobile Delta 88 that rode low to the ground as if it were built just for cruising around looking for trouble. All I needed was a ride so I could get my friends back before any of them got hurt.

After a short ride along Township Line Road, we entered Queens Village, a housing project in the West End. I could tell we were getting close to the action because I could hear people yelling. Our car windows were down and the streets there were like Driftwood Terrace; narrow, one-way streets designed to fit as many semi-detached row homes into four city blocks as they could. We were going the wrong way on a one-way street and I couldn't wait to get out of that car. I noticed the driver trying to get Matthew to take something out of the glove compartment. The driver reached across and pulled out a handgun. I'm thinking, oh shit! How the hell am I getting out of this? The driver put the gun on Sammy's lap. Sammy quickly passed it over to Matthew.

Just then, I saw Carmine, Petie, Jimmy, and Danny running towards us. They must not have recognized the car we were in because they keep running past my side of our vehicle. The look on their faces was sheer desperation. I said, "Stop the car and let us out." The driver slammed on the breaks. I started to open the car door when, all of a sudden, the guys chasing my friends saw us. They stop running after them and started to surround us. I had one foot on the ground and stopped when I saw a flash of fire and heard gunshots. Our windshield was breaking as the guys whose neighborhood we entered were throwing projectiles at us. I closed the car door and said, "Go, go, go, go!" The driver complied and I was relieved to be pulling away from this scene. I didn't look back but could hear our car being hit by hard objects as we sped away. Matthew continued to fire the gun as we sped away.

Driftwood is about a half-mile away and when we got there all of us in the back seat hurriedly exited the vehicle and in an instant, the driver and his two occupants drove away. We now needed to go to find our friends. Fortunately, we found them within minutes on Township Line Road returning to Driftwood. They were nearly out of breath and swearing that the guys from Castleton were trying to kill them by shooting a gun at them. Without telling them what we saw, we split up. Alex and Jimmy, Petie, and Carmine went home and Gunther, Danny, and I stayed at my house that night. I was upset that I allowed myself to get caught up in this. Gunther told Danny DeMarco about the shooting and he seemed to revel in it. Danny asked questions like "Did you see anyone get hit?" Gunther said, "Yes." After that, Gunther was just quiet and asked me, "Do you think anyone saw us?" At that time, I didn't care if they did. I felt guilty for being part of a person getting hurt, but I wasn't going to tell anyone what I saw. To me, it was like things happen and you can't change it, at best you can hope for is to learn from it. I knew the guy would be brought to Sacred Heart Hospital just two blocks away. And the doctors and nurses would take care of him there. What was done was done and nobody can change that.

Within a week, as Matthew returned to Fort Dix, New Jersey he was picked up by the FBI and arrested. When the police began their investigation of the shooting, the guys from the West End told them the names of the Driftwood troublemakers. A few of the notable tough guys from Driftwood like Butchy Leone and Billy Ross got picked up by the local police. The West End guys fucked up when they said names of Driftwood guys who were already in reform school, locked up in jail, or were in the service and stationed overseas. I didn't know how close the cops came to arrest me until years later when I was an adult and the subject came up and my mother said, "Did you know the detectives came to our house a couple of days after the person was shot? They asked for Jimmy and I told them he was in the Air Force serving his country in South Korea and had been there for the last six months." Jimmy was no trouble maker so the guys from the west end must have remembered his name from when he and Benny MacVee used to hang out at the Dino's hamburger joint in the west end of Castleton. The cops believed my mom and went away. At that time, my mother had no clue I was anywhere near the scene of the crime that night.

The next morning we went to the other side of Driftwood to see what was going on. A girl who I knew told me that Chucky Boyl, who was a tough guy from the West End, vouched for me. He and I played baseball together and he told the guys in his area that it would be very unlikely that I would be involved in anything like that. For the next week, rumors circled. After a while, Mom had a suspicion I was there when she heard the Volpes were looking for me.

The Volpes brought in all their forces, including Uncle Sammy. I guess they cruised Driftwood Terrace looking for people who witnessed the incident. They wanted to make sure no one was going to talk. I was no stranger to them and they knew I was in the car. A week after the incident, Fredrico Volpe saw me walking across the playground and approached me and asked me to come over to his house. He said, "We want to talk to you." I told him I didn't see anything and that I couldn't talk right now and that I would come over later. My brother Gerald was starting to hang around with Popeye and Samuel so things were not that critical. Besides, if no one said anything by now they were not going to say anything at all. The person hit by the bullet was a street guy and recovered right away, so it's not as if some innocent person was hit in a drive-by. For weeks, Fredrico continued to bug me every time I saw him. By now, Matthew was bailed out of jail and allowed to return home from Fort Dix on the weekends. Fredrico said, "Matthew's lawyer wants to talk to you. The lawyer wants to hear you say you were with him in the car and you didn't see him shoot a gun." I said I would think about it. I felt unsure of how I was going to handle my predicament. I didn't have anyone to talk to about it; because I didn't want to admit that I was involved and hurt my parents.

Fredrico approached me again about a week later. This time I said to myself, "Fuck it, just deal with it." So I said to Fredrico, "All right, what do you want?" He said, "Come over to the house; we want to talk to you about a few things." I finally gave in and went into their house.

I've walked by the front of this place a hundred times going to and from Holy Sacrament School and the backyard when I was cutting through the playground while going to the other side of Driftwood.

Their house sat up on a ridge along Hampton Road overlooking the Sun Oil Refinery. When sitting on their front porch on a clear day, you could see New Jersey. There were no steps or a walkway to access the front porch without walking up the driveway. The concrete driveway is bordered by a stone wall. This wall is about six feet high across the front and turned in on either side of the driveway. The stones are made of granite blocks slightly larger than a microwave oven. It resembled a fortress. This was the first time I was allowed in. Very few people outside the family had this opportunity. I was a little surprised to see a billiard table in the middle room but did not dare ask, where the hell do you people sit down to have dinner? I was soon to find out that there was no lawyer anywhere near that house. In the house, that day were Matthew, the old man, Uncle Sammy, Anthony,

Samuel, Salvatore, Popeye, and assorted kids running around everywhere. And, of course, the pain in my ass, Fredrico, was leading me into the kitchen at the other end of the first floor. Fredrico asked me to sit down at their small kitchen table. Popeye was milling around the sink pretending to be doing something. Samuel and Matthew and the rest stayed in the front rooms.

Fredrico said, "We want you to go to court with Matthew. But first, we want to see if the prosecuting attorney can get you to say something that is not good for us." I was thinking to myself, if someone as smart as a lawyer treats me right while asking me questions, I'm going to tell them everything and let the chips fall where they may. As far as I was concerned, it was in God's hands. I was there and Matthew did shoot a gun that night, so deal with it. Of course, I didn't say that there. But if I received a subpoena to go to court, that's exactly what was going to happen.

Just then, Marie walked through the kitchen and gave me this look that said, "You're in deep shit boy and I feel sorry for you." And I gave her a look back that said, "Girl, you are absolutely right." Fredrico asked if I saw anything the night of the shooting and who else was in the back seat. I told him I wasn't sure what I saw. Just flashes in the night and I didn't know if they were shooting at us or not. I did see some guys throwing rocks at our car and our front windshield was shattered at the time. The sounds of hard things were hitting the side of the vehicle. I also told him who was in the back with me. At this time, I thought it really didn't matter because I figured any one of them would tell, just as I was doing.

A court date was set and my parents decided to go for a drive down to Fort Lauderdale. They took everyone in the family from me on down with them. We came back in a week because school was about to start. The court date for Mathew was postponed and finally, a plea bargain was made. I heard that Mathew and the driver of the car were both fined for discharging a firearm within city limits and disturbing the peace. ✂

# Chapter 9: Return To Normal

After September things returned to normal and my young girlfriend Sally and I went our separate ways. She was a good girl but we just didn't have the right chemistry. I had a few girlfriends after her. Mostly if a girl said she liked me, I would say I liked her, too. That sounds simple, but not just any girl would take the chance to come out and say they liked you. Mostly everyone knows who should date who. It was customary to start with a girlfriend of hers asking, "Do you like so and so or not?" They would ask me and I would say yes or no. If it was no, her response was, "Well she didn't really want to date you anyway."

Once I said no regarding a local girl named Helen. Since one of her friends was going out with my friend Petie and another was going out with my friend Jimmy, the girls thought it would be convenient if Helen and I went out too. To my negative response, Helen's friend came back with a bargaining chip; she said, "If you do go out with her she won't let you go all the way, but you can finger her." I politely declined. I did not want to go out with a girl that would bargain with her virginal cavity. Well, it didn't end there; it just so happened that Helen's mother and mine worked together at the hospital. They must have talked about me and Helen's possible relationship because my mom asked me why I didn't want to go out with Helen. My answer to my mom was referring to my younger sister, saying, "Helen looks too much like Joan." My Mom just said, "Phillip you're crazy, get the hell out of here."

Typically, when one of us did get hooked up with a girl, we would meet at the dance and have a good time with our guy friends and end up finding our girlfriends for slow dances. It worked out because when the fast songs came on and we didn't feel like dancing we could stand around and look cool while watching the girls dance with each other. Then when a slow song came on you had someone to dance and share the mood with. The last dance was always the same old song, "Hold me, Thrill me, Kiss me" sung by Mel Carter. After that, we would walk our girl home. The dances were the highlight of our week. We were regulars there and nobody bothered us. There were about 80 people each Friday night and the DJ gave a solid mix of fast and slow songs and we had no complaints. The Isley Brothers and Delphonics were popular at the time. Grazing in the Grass by Hugh Masekela was particularly easy to dance to. About midway through the night they would hold a dance contest and the winner was decided by the applause from the spectators, usually, the drunkest of us would enter and whoever did the craziest moves won. Every once in a while when requested our DJ would let someone from the crowd come up and sing along with a record. This was way before Karaoke became popular in the U.S. so instead of Karaoke we called it. "Look some asshole is up on stage trying to sing."

Before we went to the dance a couple of friends and I would meet on the corner of Market and Hampton to scrounge up a couple of dollars. Then we would find one of the older guys from the neighborhood - someone old enough to buy beer, like my brother Jimmy. We'd ask them to go to the tavern and buy us some beer. All we could afford was a six-pack of Schmitt's beer. We'd usually split it amongst three guys and we would get blasted. After drinking our fill of beer, we would go to the dance. I was known as, "Two beers Phil" and Petie was known as, "One beer Pete". At seventeen, we were easy drunks. We would do silly things like going up on stage to sing a Smokey Robinson and the Miracles song. On one occasion, I was Smokey and Gunther and Danny were the Miracles. We had to share one microphone and by the second chorus, we were on the floor wrestling over the microphone. Another time, Petie walked around the dance floor kissing any girl who would let him, no matter how homely they were. Our other acquaintances would see this behavior and question, "How many beers did he have," and the answer was always ONE.

One fateful night at the dance, I was pissed off because we couldn't get someone to buy us beer. Then I saw this Black guy gritting at me. Gritting is when someone you don't know gives you a mean glare. Usually, I would just look back at them, letting the person know I wasn't a punk and then look away in disgust. There were very few Blacks coming to the dance and most of the time they were cool and no one I knew cared whether they were there or not. This night I said to him, "What the hell are you looking at nigger?" He heard me and right away I regretted what I said. Not because I was afraid of him or that I just hurt the feelings of a nice guy, but because I always tried to avoid being racist. He came over to me and said, "What the fuck did you say, honky?" At this time security came and told both of us to leave. He was with a friend and I was with Gunther Price. All four of us walked up the block and down an alley until we got behind Wilson's drug store. He and I started to have a fistfight. It wasn't a very exciting fight because neither of us was very mean spirited. I'd seen him around the Black section of Upper Manchester. And I knew he didn't go to Man, but instead he went to a school for troubled youth. The fight was more like tag with our fist. He was my height but outweighed me by twenty "fat" pounds. I couldn't let him grab a hold of me so I just jabbed him in the face and he tagged me a couple of times with his fat fist, but the fight wasn't very aggressive. I reached into back my pocket to pull out a small ½ by four-inch long pipe that I kept on me in case I ever got jumped. I was going to put it in my fist like a roll of dimes and hit him hard enough to stop the fight. He saw me doing this and took a step back and said, "No knives, no knives." He thought that I was pulling a knife on him. I wasn't carrying a knife. And the thought never crossed my mind. So I just stuffed the pipe back into my pocket. We stood back and we looked at each other. His partner who was smaller but more aggressive said, "I can kick your ass, you white mother fucker." As he stepped towards me, Gunther stepped in and those two started to fight. Well, they were doing a hell of a lot better job at fighting than us, my past opponent and I just stood back and watched real street fighters in action. These guys must have both been abused somehow because they were punching, wrestling, and rolling on the ground. Each one was trying to choke the other. I was thinking I should stop calling people names and give up fighting because compared to these guys, I suck at it. All of a sudden my brother Gerald came by and said, "The cops are coming." I looked up to see a police car coming down the alley and we all ran in different directions.

Around eleven p.m., I returned to the dance and saw Gunther standing in the middle of the street directly in front of the firehouse. Close to him was this older, taller Black guy I did not recognize. Stopped in the middle of the street, were what looked like three cars full of Blacks. I was compelled by friendship to go over to see what was up. Gunther said, in a very direct and curious way, "Have you seen Phil Webster lately? This guy says he pulled a knife on his cousin?" Without hesitation and as smooth as I could, I said, "No, I haven't seen him all night." At this time, the guy I had been fighting got out of the last car. I am thinking, "Oh shit! What the hell am I going to do now?"

Miraculously, at the same time, the dance let out. First out of the firehouse door were the bouncers, followed by about 80 White people. We all know the fact that only about ten of those White people would actually be brave enough to get into a street fight against these Blacks so, lucky for us, the Blacks saw this happening and turned, got back in their cars, and drove away. Gunther and I were very glad to be relieved of our situation. I didn't realize how bad the situation was until Gunther told me that the guy talking to him in the street had a six-inch knife with the blade pressed up against his ribs.

The next Monday at school, my brother Gerald heard a couple of Black guys say that after the next period when I came into the bathroom they were going to jump me. Typically, between each class period, smokers would go into the restrooms to catch a couple of puffs of a cigarette. And I was one of them. Before I got there, Gerald told them that if any one of them touched me he would make them pay for it. I walked into that boy's room and no one said a word to me. I didn't even know about what was said until my brother told me weeks later. I guess I was still under that blanket.

A couple of weeks later things started to change. Some guy wanted to date Alice Carr and my brother John said she was a "pig" for going out with him. John and Alice had continued their platonic relationship since the first grade. Well, what John said got back to this guy and he was telling everyone that he was going to kick John's ass. I should have figured out that the person telling me this just wanted to see me get in a fight with this guy. And, of course, the guy talking trash about my brother John just happened to show up at the dance ten minutes later. I went up to him and asked if I could talk to him outside. Before we passed the exit, we both got our hand stamped as if we were coming right back. We went outside to the alley in the back of the firehouse and we talked. See, everyone knew who could take who. And everyone knew that I could take this guy. And everyone knew that he could kick John's ass. He also had an older brother in a motorcycle gang so I guess he thought he had a reputation to uphold. I told him that I couldn't allow someone to talk about kicking my brother's ass. He said that he liked Alice and could not let someone talk bad about her. I told him about how long John and Alice knew each other. And that John was only acting as if he was her big brother. He accepted what I said. I told him that I would talk to John about saying stuff about him and Alice. He then said he would not threaten my brother so we shook hands and re-entered the dance. It was a turn for the better in my interpersonal relationships. Gone are the days of me saying crap like, "If that guy said something like that about anyone I cared about I'd punch his face in or call people racist names." And of course, I never said a word to my brother John about what had happened.

About two months later I got a new girlfriend named Katie Meadows. She was way too pretty for me. To this day I don't know why she liked me. She went to Man High with us but was a year behind me and in academic classes so I hardly ever saw her. All of my buddies were jealous when they found out she wanted to date me. I wasn't about to say no when her friend asked if I wanted to meet her. She looked like she could be a princess of some Scandinavian country. She was a very nice, calm person. She and I would do the same thing as everyone else. We'd greet each other at the beginning of the dance, say "Hi", hug, and then go our separate ways to hang out with our friends. We would get together for the slow dances and walk home together. Believe it or not, she lived in dirty old Penn's Port.

After two pleasant weeks of dating, while walking her home we passed some of the Volpes and a couple of their friends including my brother Jerald hanging on the street corner. I wasn't worried about them, but that is not the case for a girl that's from another neighborhood. As far as she was concerned, the only thing she knew about them was their notorious reputation. So I wasn't surprised that she was a little intimidated. One of them yelled to us in a mock threatening way, "Where do you think you're going?" Another said, "Give me a cigarette." I didn't answer them because I knew they weren't serious. But all she knew was that a bunch of older guys hanging on the corner were trying to bother us and that we had to walk past them. I didn't think anything of it or I would have told her who Gerald was. As we were crossing the Penn's Port Bridge about midway, two Black guys came up the steps from the Amtrak train station and were following about twenty feet behind us and walking at a faster pace. Not a problem; there were plenty of Blacks living in Penn's Port and we knew most of them. Penn's Port was about 90% White and 10% Black and we all went to the same junior and senior high schools. Well, believe it or not, it was that fat guy I had the fight with about three months earlier. Katie knew of the near race riot that almost started from our fight, so when they caught up to us at the foot of the bridge, I stepped her to the side and turned her towards me so my back was to them and we kissed. They just walked past us by like we weren't even there. She was thoroughly rattled by now and had enough for one night. She said, "I want to walk home alone from here," it was about four blocks from her house but she insisted. I was a little worried about her. It was nearing midnight in Penn's Port but she insisted. So I dejectedly watched her as she walked down the street and rounded the corner.

It was normal for a couple dating not to see each other until the next weekend, especially early in a relationship. I didn't see her until the next Friday night at the firehouse dance. She arrived late and avoided me. I asked her friend, "What's the problem with Kate?" She said, "Katie can't see you anymore." Immediately, I walked over to Katie and asked what the problem was. Her friend said, "Look what you did to her." Without saying a word Katie pulled down the front of her shirt to expose the top portion of her chest. That's when I saw this big red rash. She said, "My doctor said I should break up with you." Well, I would rather she tell me that she kissed my brother or that my breath smelled like decaying teeth. Instead, she said that her nerves caused this. How in the hell was I going to fight that? I just turned and walked away sitting down for the rest of the night. I could only sit and watch as an acquaintance started "hitting" on her. I decided to just cool it with the chicks for a while.

One evening, Gunther and I were loitering on the corner of Hampton and Market streets in front of Romeo's Hoagie shop. Alice Carr drove by in her new Chevy Chevelle Supersport; a gift her father bought her for her 18th birthday. The weather changed to a light sprinkle as she pulled over and asked if we wanted to ride around with her. I knew her because she was John's friend, but I don't know if Gunther had ever met her before. Gunther got in the back seat first and me in the front seat. We talked some small talk but nothing special as she drove around Driftwood. After a few trips up and down Market Street and Manchester Avenue, she headed towards Upper Man. We ended up in a quiet neighborhood and she pulled over and parked the car. I was thinking I would rather stay down in Driftwood. To my surprise, Alice got out of her two-door car and got into the back seat with Gunther. I don't have a clue as to what brought this on; maybe a message sent through some telepathic vibe or a wiggle of an ear. I never heard a thing and if I was the only one in the car with her we would be sitting there looking out the window talking about the weather. Well, they started to pull down their pants and I realized what was going on. I was in a state of astonishment and wondered what I should do. What was the proper etiquette in a situation like this? It started to rain so I didn't want to get out and get wet or walk around an unfamiliar street and have some old lady call the cops on me. Maybe I missed some eye contact or some code word that says please excuse us while we fuck. So I just sat there as they proceeded to have intercourse in the back seat of the new car her daddy just bought her. I didn't have to look to know what was happening. But I couldn't resist taking one quick little peek at them just to take a mental snapshot. The sights, sounds, and smells are very distinctive. The rest of the time I looked around to see if anyone was walking by. I started to think even if somebody came nearby they couldn't see anything through these steamed up windows. The action in the back seat didn't last long. When he finished, my friend wanted to get out of the back seat. Since it was a two-door I got out of the car in order to let him out. When I did, he motioned to Alice and said, "Go ahead, Phil." Alice was still lying with her short little legs up in the air; exposing her La La as an open invitation to me. I did not find this appealing in the very least, so I said, "No thank you." With that answer she pulled up her pants, got back in the driver's seat, Gunther hopped back into the back seat, and we proceeded back to Driftwood.

Strange things seemed to happen around Romeo's Sandwich Shop. On one cold evening, about five of us went inside the store to hang out. In the winter we would hang out there to stay warm. All hoagie shops in that area had pinball machines for the customers to play while waiting for their sandwiches to be made. We liked to watch people play. It was cheap entertainment. We didn't have any money, except for Carmine, and he would have about fifty cents his mommy would give him. He was one of those kids whose mother let him smoke cigarettes in the house at the age of thirteen. She would give him money for just being her baby boy. He was seven minutes younger than his twin Danny. We would mostly just hang out and watch him play pinball. Popeye Volpe was only eighteen at the time and worked at Romeo's. Popeye was drinking a vanilla milkshake that he made for himself. Danny asked Popeye for a swig of his milkshake. Danny should have known better because after he asked him the third time, without a blink of an eye, Popeye pulled out his doodle and stuck it into his own milkshake and asked Danny if he wanted some now. We laughed our asses off. Popeye was sticking the drink near Danny's lips and teasing him with it. Popeye then threw the drink in the sink and told all of us begging, scroungy dogs to get the hell out of the store before he kicked all of our asses. ❧

## Chapter 10: Going Too Far

The next year I was at a party and I was hanging out with a girl named Jackie Pruitt. Later her friend asked if I liked her and if we were going to start going out together. She was ok, just not my cup of tea. I knew Marie Volpe was going out with a guy who was no good for her and cheated on her. So I took a chance and said no to this girl. When they asked why I didn't want to go out with Jackie, I said, "Because, I like Marie Volpe." I knew that if I said that the subject would be closed. Besides, I really did like Marie; I just didn't like some of the things she was doing. She was going out with older guys, drinking, doing drugs, and beating up girls who happened to like the same guy she liked. Word got back to Marie about what I told the other girl. So, when I saw her the next Friday night, I asked her to slow dance with me and she did.

"Mariearella" had found her freedom. Her old man worked in his pizza shop in Castleton until after 11:30 pm when it closed. This gave her until midnight to get in the house before he came home. Marie would go to school, come home, clean the house, cook dinner for her family, and do the dishes before she could go out. I don't have a clue what her mother was doing. Again the next week Marie and I met at the Friday night dance and talked. The guy she had a crush on was there but it didn't seem to matter. His time of using her was over. She seemed to like spending time with me.

Marie and I were born one year apart. I was older but she was still physically more mature and much worldlier than I. It was around this time that I was slowly catching up to her. I was five foot eleven inches tall and 145 lbs and in my second year of puberty. Marie was a perfect five foot six and 130 lbs. She still had that long black wavy hair that agreed with her, "I don't give a shit," attitude. She looked her best without any makeup and wore hip hugger bell-bottom blue jeans and a pullover shirt and no underwear. I would wear khaki paints (also known as Castleton bags) and a pullover dark blue sweatshirt and always, tighty-whities. In the winter, she wore a nice heavy overcoat her brother Mathew bought her. And I wore a full-length brown suede coat. I was very proud of that coat because I was able to buy it with my own money. I earned a dollar an hour for washing dishes at the Rubies Dinner in Penn's Port. I would work from eleven p.m. until eight a.m. every Friday and Saturday night. After three months, I was able to save enough money to buy my coat for seventy dollars. I purchased the coat in November and wore it all the time. I was very careful not to spill any beer on it.

On a very cold January night in 1971, Marie and I walked home together from the dance for the first time. We waited so we could dance to "Hold Me, Thrill Me, Kiss Me" before we left. She lived about three blocks away from the firehouse but we could walk through Driftwood school's playground and cut the distance in half. She could go through her backyard when it was time for her to go in. We paused to talk before saying goodnight and sat on a telephone pole that was lying down on the ground acting as a barrier to the playground and her back fence, but on this night, it was our intimate couch. We talked for about five minutes. This didn't please her as she was expecting a lot more from a guy who was alone with her. She said, "If it's going to be like this, I'm going in." It was getting colder and she only had so much time that night. I said, "Marie don't go yet." She decided to give me another chance. In spite of her mind-set and the smell of wine on her breath, I gave her a long deep kiss. All that I said was, "Sweet dreams and have a good night, Marie." She just looked me in the eyes for a long warm second and ran into her house.

The next Friday, we met and sat down and watched the people dance. She began to act very strangely and talked about seeing light trails and vivid colors. She then waved her hand in front of her face and said, "Wow!" This behavior grossed me out and I told her that we should go outside and talk. When we got outside we began to walk towards her house; her demeanor seemed strange as if she was on autopilot. As we reached her backyard she didn't want to sit down and talk. I was starting to suspect that she took a hit of acid; LSD Lysergic acid - an illegal psychedelic drug. I've never taken any kind of drugs before, but I was pretty sure what this was. I asked her what she took and she said, "Acid, I got it from Bonnie, a friend of hers that came from a whole family of drug addicts. It upset me that some of my friends and thousands of hippies were turning to hallucinogenic drugs and it really upset me that Marie was partaking in this mind-altering behavior. I tried to talk to her about why I didn't like hard drugs. I told her what my mom would tell us, "If you took illicit drugs no matter how much money or education you acquired, you would always be lower class. And that dope users were selfish and are no use to anyone, not even themselves." I also told her how she was too good of a person to do this to herself. I told her that her little brothers and sisters were counting on her to take care of them. She didn't seem to be getting it. She just said I was a "bummer." With that comment, I decided that I had enough and I gave her a little kiss on the forehead and said, "Goodbye, Marie." She looked me in the eyes for a long cold second and turned and walked away. I watched as she went into her house thinking that this relationship wasn't going to work.

The next day, my younger sister, Mary and her friend asked if I was going to start dating Marie. I told them that I was not if she took any kind of drugs. The word got back to Marie. I don't know what it took on her part, because she made a very mature decision that week and came to the dance only high on wine. She came to me and asked for the last dance. I said, "Yes, of course." She was sixteen and I was seventeen and we were together and all was right in our world.

The next Saturday, we walked down to the Mall. It wasn't far, only about two or three miles. I liked to walk and talk about all kinds of things. She liked to listen. She lived in a closed, controlled environment and no one told her about the outside world. We got along well. We never talked down to each other. She put the Wonder in "WE" and I put in the Explanation. I grew up around relatively smart people and I would listen to them as they talked to each other. Sure, when I was younger my brother John would give me a smart-aleck answer to some of my questions, but someone listening would correct him for me.

Marie and I went to a movie that cold January afternoon, I don't remember what the movie was; I think it was "Patton." Afterward, we stopped in a Hoagie shop and split a hoagie sandwich before walking home. It was getting late by then and kind of cold and we were warm from walking, but both getting a little tired. When we got to the bottom of her family's driveway we stopped and got into her brother's car to take a break and say goodnight. Time slipped by and neither of us had a watch to tell exactly what time it was. Marie began to get anxious and must have sensed that her old man was about to come home. She began to open the car door when I stopped her to give her a goodnight kiss; that is when a car's headlights beamed straight on us. Someone stopped their car before turning up into the driveway. I looked to see who it was and, sure enough, it was her old man and two of her brothers. Marie became really scared and got out of the car to run in the house, but it was too late. The old man got out of his car and began to approach us. She skirted along the far side of the driveway trying her best to avoid a smack in the back of the head. Her old man was yelling at her as if she had committed the worse sin in the world. He said, "Get your fucking ass into that house and you better stay there too."

Well until then, I've never heard an adult say fuck before. Then he said, "You're not allowed out for a year." I was taken aback by his abrupt anger but I was able to say, "Mr. Volpe, did you say a year?" He was so mad at me that he didn't even look at me and stuttered when he said, "Maybe not a year but three weeks." It was surreal. I just turned and walked away. Luckily her brothers stayed in the car and did not support their old man in his tirade.

Life in the Webster's house didn't change a lot. My mom still worked the graveyard shift at the hospital. When she was happy, she sang show tunes, "People Who Need People Are the Luckiest People in the World." And when she was sad she would say, "Tell me something good, will you, Phillip." I never did. I wish I could think of something to cheer her up, but I couldn't. My gift to my mother was to believe her when she acted happy but, regretfully, I couldn't give her happiness when she was blue.

Dad assumed the duties of helping the family with their daily needs. He drove everyone to their jobs, washed clothes, cooked dinner, and went to the store. Typically, when I came home late something was saved for me. The last one to eat always knew who they were. If someone didn't have dinner yet, they would let you know by saying, "Save something for Ann or Gerald." Nana washed dishes and cleaned around the house. Elizabeth was still in the convent. Ann held her job at the hospital in spite of going out with Petie to all hours of the night. Katherine kept her job and helped to support the family. James was still in the Air Force and back from South Korea and was now stationed in South Carolina. John got a job at the Franklin Mint and bought himself a used car. Gerald graduated and got a job at the Castleton Shipyard. Although as soon as my older brothers graduated from high school they put in applications in the refineries for work, not one of them was able to get hired into Sun Oil or British Petroleum's refineries. It was tough living so close to the refinery that you could smell the dank odor of oil heating up and the constant hissing sound of steam being released from a valve. Sometimes this huge fireball came from the nearby burnoff tower and would suddenly appear with an associated rumbling noise that you hoped would not explode. This ball of fire could be seen for miles. Of all the families on Cole and Claremont Streets with fathers working at Sun Oil, not a single boy or girl for that matter got a job there. When it came to my turn in 1972 the refineries weren't even taking applications anymore.

I was in the eleventh grade at Man High and Mary was in the tenth grade also at Man High. Joan, Kevin, Ruth, and Holly were still going to Holy Sacrament. Mary started to date Dave Rose, one of the guys I was hanging around with. I didn't like it at first, but he was an all right guy and I never heard him say a bad word about any of his earlier girlfriends, so I looked the other way.

That year I was introduced to boxing. In spite of my convictions towards the sport of football, I liked boxing. I think it's because I was maturing and wanted to show that I was a good fighter without anyone getting hurt. To be sure no one was injured; I went to the sporting goods store and bought 16-ounce gloves (the pros use eight to ten-ounce gloves.) I did very well for myself. Dave Rose was my closest competitor. He was very good at counter punching. If I hit him with a left jab, he was able to return the favor. The same thing happened with a lower strike to the midsection. It made me to not want to hit him anymore. I always knew if it came down to a real fight since I outweighed him by ten pounds, I could just grab him and take him down. Besides, I never threw my right cross very often. I didn't feel as though I could use that punch fast enough to connect without it hitting my opponent hard. I didn't want to hurt anyone.

Marie's brother, Samuel, tried to box me, but I had the reach on him and was able to keep him away by sticking out my left jab and moving my feet to stay out away from him. Normally we would spar out in the playground but one time it was raining so we went under the Penn's Port Bridge at the foot of Green Street. It was here that I was challenged by this Black guy who everyone knew had a crush on Marie. She could not stand him and everyone there knew it. He was always hanging out with Samuel or Popeye. He didn't have a lot going for him. He was a year older, but I was taller and more athletic. I was able to outscore him with my jab and block most of his attempts to hit me. This embarrassed and frustrated him into losing all technique and "bum" rushing in and trying to maul me by making contact with my face with his arms and elbows. I was able to survive, but I sensed that this sparring was more than just a friendly match for the sport of it. After this encounter, I put the gloves away for good.

Marie had my phone number and after a couple of days she called me and before you knew it, she and I were back spending time together. After about eight weeks of seeing each other, I gave her a blue star sapphire ring. I never asked her if she wanted to go steady. I said, "Marie I bought you this ring, do you want to wear it?" She said, "Yes if you want me to."

After seeing each other for about three months she started to babysit her brother, Anthony's four kids at his house. She invited me to go with her, so I did. Anthony (pronounced Ant-Nee) and his wife Judy (pronounced Jew- D) belonged to a bowling league on Wednesday night and on Saturday evenings they spent the evening at a nightclub. Anthony lived in the west end of Castleton on the other side of Highland Avenue from where we had the gang fight. Anthony lived there since before the fight and nobody messed with him, so I wasn't worried too much when we went up there. Marie and I took care of the kids. They were well behaved with us around. Marie was a 'natural' with children. She never had to holler or even try to trick or bribe them into doing what she asked. She would put them upstairs in bed around nine o'clock. That left us alone downstairs to do as we pleased. As soon as we figured that the kids were safe and sound, we would start to kiss. I liked that and so did she. After a couple of hours or so her brother Anthony would come home and he would drive us back to Driftwood. Marie told me that of all her older brothers, only Anthony said anything nice about me. He told her that he thought I was a good guy and to keep a hold of me. We didn't put any pressure on each other to take our relationship any farther sexually and I was fine with that. After a couple of months we were hanging out in the playground and I asked her if she thought we would still be going out in the summer. She said, "No."

After about five months of going steady, we would take our kissing and making out pretty far. I didn't know much about sex but I did see the cartoon character Popeye the Sailorman kiss Olive Oil, up and down her arm so I tried it on Marie and she liked it. I also like to suck on her titties; she liked when I did this very much. She would pull my shirt over her head and kiss my stomach and chest. I liked this too. We would stick our tongues in each other's belly button and kiss each other's bare chest. It became harder and harder to stop, but we did. While we were making out like this I wasn't worried about anything that I know now should have worried me. Since I'd never had sexual intercourse before, the one thing that worried me was that since the physical act of sexual intercourse has such unique movements, what if when we started to have intercourse and as I was pumping away, would my ass muscles give out before I was done? Or worse yet, get an ass muscle spasm and she thinks I am having an orgasm and gets disappointed in me and wants to quit. The only time I had an orgasm was in a wet dream and it was over before I woke up. I tried masturbating once but became embarrassed with myself and stopped.

The next time we went up to her brother's house to watch the kids, we started where we left off; except this time after she put the kids to bed, I met her at the bottom of the stairs. We started to kiss each other all over our mouths and chests. We pulled up our tops and unbuttoned our pants so we could get an all flesh feeling when we French kissed each other's belly buttons. I felt as though I had a statuette of Mr. Universe posing in the front of my pants. I didn't want it to hit her chin so I pulled her up and we kissed each other's lips. We were going to do what I always knew we were going to do. That certain part of the male's anatomy was prepared for it's coming out party. The purpose for its present state is going to be realized. It could no longer wait. We went upstairs to her brothers and sister in law's bed. We continued to do what we started on the bottom stairs. I lay on top of her kissing her lips and neck and her kissing mine. We removed each other's tops and I started to suck on her breast. Her nipples decided to come out farther than they ever did before and this was an added treat. We pulled down each other's pants just far enough so she could open up her legs for me and we continue with this act of pleasing each other. I was as ready as I could be and there was no stopping us now. The aroma in the room contributed to the pleasure. I was right where I wanted to be. I did not have a care in the world. The only thing that mattered was Phillip and Marie satisfying a desire that seemed as if it was building for a lifetime. I entered her as if we were made for each other. At entrance, we both produced a sound through our noses that expressed our pleasure. I began to stroke the inside of her vagina with my penis as if I had done this a thousand times. All my previous worries had vanished. She started to move in rhythm with me as she inserted her tongue in my mouth. With each stroke, the pleasure grew. My doodle had found its home, it's very own warm and snug enclosure. There was no one else in the world except us. When I realized what we were doing, I reached another echelon of excitement. This put me on a course to extreme pleasure. I began to think about my ass muscles giving out, but that wasn't going to happen because this was going to end real soon. I was able to stop from kissing for a second and concentrate on the pending eruption below. I needed to regain some control of myself before I unloaded a piece of my soul inside her. As I was reaching the point of no return, I did a pushup lifting the upper portion of my body off hers and without using my hands I withdrew and lay my testicles on her labia. The root of my doodle landed on the mound of her vagina. I continued to pump one more time. As I did this the seeds of my ancestors were released unto the world. This unleashing lasted until I became anesthetized down there and stopped pumping. I looked down and saw my seeds lying harmlessly outside our bodies causing no worries past the cleaning up of the sheets and the headboard. Then for a few seconds, I collapsed on top of her in a state of pure contentment and peace. After about twenty relaxing seconds we collected ourselves and remade the bed, washed up and went downstairs.

About an hour later, Anthony came home as usual and drove us back to Driftwood. We went to our separate beds for a good night's sleep. When you first meet someone you truly care about it seems as if it takes forever to see them again. You do your routine things in a half-interested fashion. When I made love to her she became part of my life. Nothing was done without thinking of her. I could not wait to be with the person who shared that intimacy with me. And it was satisfying knowing that I made her feel that way too.

Finally, the next weekend arrived and we were at it again. That night we did it three times. The first time it was over in about thirty seconds. The second time we made love. I did it the right way because before my ass muscles gave out she entered into this state of what I call "temporary insanity." I wasn't sure what was happening at first, but I soon figured out she was having an orgasm. Not once, but twice within about ten minutes. I figured what it was the second time and it compelled me to join her. I was able to collect myself before I did something really insane and unload inside her. I always wondered what the Catholics called the "Rhythm Method" and now I know. It's when you are about to have an orgasm inside someone that you don't want to get pregnant. You keep pumping and stroking the inside of her vagina with your doodle until you get this feeling of no return. You then pull out just as you are about to ejaculate. If it only takes one pump on her mound after you withdraw to ejaculate (look mom no hands) you got the correct "Rhythm." After only a few times, I got really good at it. It was as if I was doing it all my life. I could almost withdraw and release at will. The third time we did it that night at Anthony's was for the fun of it. We were standing face to face having sex in front of the kitchen sink while I was looking out the window to see if her brother was coming home.

Marie and I babysat a lot. Once we babysat for one of Anthony's friends, Bruce Pride. Since he was a combatant in Viet Nam, he thought he was cool, but he wasn't cool, even a little bit. He seemed to me as if he is condescending to any male not an army combatant. Unlike most combat veterans, he told me a tale about how he and Marie's brother, Matthew, were in the same platoon and how they had a firefight holding off the Viet Cong. He was saying how he would fire his 50 cal machine gun. He paused to explain how you are supposed to fire the gun in spurts, that way; you don't heat the barrel up too much. He continued to say, "But later for that, when the gooks are coming, you don't stop to think about anything. You just keep firing away." God love and bring peace to all our war veterans, but this guy needed to settle down.

Bruce knew my sister Ann's boyfriend El Dorado Pete from Castleton and he knew Pete's business and that my sister Ann was dating him. Pete worked outside the law. He was what people in that world called a "Ten-Percenter." He was German and French but most of the organized crime people he worked with were Italian and, because he was an "earner," they liked him. The top organized crime guy around was his protector. So this meant nobody should even consider messing with him. A Ten-Percenter always has a lot of cash on hand because he needed it in his dealings. Among other things, if a person won a lot of money at the racetrack and didn't want to claim it on his taxes, Petie would cash it for them and keep ten percent. This guy knew Petie carried his money and that he kept his gun in the trunk of his car. So this nut takes me in the living room and tells me about his brilliant idea.

He said to me, "Petie comes over to your house to pick up your sister, right?"

I said, "Sometimes."

He said, "Next time he stops in, asked him for the keys to his car, alright?"

He sees me take a step back as he continued to say, "Tell him that you just want to see what it feels like to sit and start up a Cadillac El Dorado, right?"

I interject and say, "Excuse me, but he doesn't come in the house, he pulls up, out in front of the house, blows his car's horn and my sister runs out, gets in his car, and they ride away."

He says, "He never came into your house?"

I said, "No, not with Nana around, he wouldn't dare."

Well, this asshole doesn't get it, but I don't care. He is persistent with his grand scheme and I don't know what to say.

He says, "Louie's kid is there right?" It bothered me a lot that he spoke of Holly.

I said, "Yes, she is."

He says, "You must have some Play-Doh around the house right?"

He keeps saying right as if he wants me to fall into this pattern of agreeing with him.

I say, "Maybe."

He said, "Just get the keys any way you can and make an impression of them on the Play-Doh and give the Play-Doh to me, I'll do the rest. And remember this, if you tell anyone what I said, I'll kill you."

Well, this is not the first time this guy threatened me. The first time was a week earlier when we first started to babysit for him and his wife. It was just before he was walking out his front door with his wife. He laid three one hundred dollar bills on top of the TV. As he did this, he looked at me, and said, "If that money is not there when I get back, I'll know it was you and I'll kill you." I didn't know what to do about asshole Bruce's plan. If I tell Ann what he said about Petie and the Play-Doh plan and she tells Petie it might get back to the bosses. And if it does, this guy is getting a severe beating before the week is out. As I understood the way they work in the world these guys live in, they can't afford to have someone outside the group hurt someone under their protection. Lucky for me, Marie knew what to do. See, in families like hers, the men sit in one room and talk about illegal stuff; the women stay in an adjacent room just within earshot, but not too close to annoy the men. His wife and Marie were good at that. Marie heard the whole thing and told Anthony the next day. After that, we never babysat for that jerk again.

Now, when I talk about these people remember they are not very big men. Maybe they were five feet six or seven inches tall, 160 pounds. The biggest one of Marie's brothers was Matthew and he was just 5' 7" and 200 lbs. After returning home from the Army he gained about forty pounds, mostly fat. I learned from watching these guys that, it's not the size of the dog in the fight, it's the size of the fight in the dog, and these guys were pit bulls.

After Marie and I had been going together for a while there was a truce between me and her family. There was always an uncomfortable atmosphere of mistrust between me and her brothers. They were the criminals and, ironically, I was the one that lacked "trust." One Sunday evening after dinner, her brother, Popeye, went out to get cigarettes, so we went for the ride just to get out of the stuffy house for awhile. We ran into Anthony passed out drunk sitting in the driver's seat of his car that was parked on the street near the bottom of their driveway. Marie was afraid that he would start the car and drive drunk so she got out and asked if he would like to go with us to get smokes. He did and he got into the back seat and quickly fell asleep.

On the way back, Popeye was taking the long way back along 10th Street in Penn's Port. We saw a guy walking along the road trying to hitch a ride. On one side of the road are twin homes and the other is the old Sinclair Oil Refinery now owned and operated by British Petroleum (BP). Well, this guy was leisurely sticking his thumb out for a ride. When Popeye noticed him he slowed down to pick the hitchhiker up. Just as the man started to open the door, Popeye stepped on the gas and we took off. The guy got pissed and smacked the side of the car and yelled something at us. This woke Anthony up and he angrily asked. "What the hell was that?" Before Marie or I could say a word Popeye said, "That guy just hit our car." Anthony said, "Turn the car around."

I looked back to see the guy with his fist in the air waving it at us. We were about 100 yards ahead by the time our car came to a sudden stop. The guy seeing this started to cross the street and headed towards the houses on the other side of the street. This guy was no slouch; he was at least six feet tall and two hundred pounds. As we approached the man, Popeye pulled over and stopped the car. Anthony got out of the car and walked directly towards the man. The man seeing this holds his arms out with open hand pleading, "Stop. I didn't do anything to you," this did not phase Anthony at all and he proceeded to beat the living shit out of the poor guy. Some of the residents came out of their houses to see what the commotion was about. Among them was what looked like a mother and her adult daughter. The younger female began hollering at Anthony to stop or she would call the cops. Popeye said to them, "You fucking bitches better shut the fuck up or you will be next." The woman and her daughter just stood on their porch and shut up. I just sat there thinking, "I can't believe this just happened." I didn't try to stop him or anything. I was just a witness. Anthony wore himself out and Popeye gave the poor guy a kick in the face just for good measure. Both got back in the car and we drove back to Driftwood to rejoin the family for a Sunday evening relaxation.

This was not the first time I was around when Anthony punched someone. One night we were babysitting and he came home drunk and was fighting with his wife Judy. He was in some stupid jealous rage. They carried the argument into the house and in total disrespect to Judy, Marie, and me, he pushed his wife into the kitchen and punched her in the nose. It made me sick and I just looked down at the floor as he passed by us to go upstairs. Marie asked Judy if she was all right and said she would be fine. Marie said, "We're going home now." In spite of it being past 2 a.m., we walked home from the west end of Castleton to Driftwood. We just needed to get the hell out of there.

I felt weak and cowardly for not doing something. It was a little more than a two-mile walk before we reached our homes. We walked it a couple of times before when he came home too drunk to drive us. He would just say let me lay down for a minute and I will take you home after I get some rest. He didn't care about driving drunk; he was just too tired and didn't want to. He would not wakeup to drive us home and everyone was too afraid to wake him. A few of times instead of driving us home, he would take Judy upstairs and fuck her very loudly and then go to sleep. Marie and I would stay the night. My mom would not like it when I did this. I understood my mom's feelings and agreed with her but she did not know the consequences of waking Anthony up when he was drunk; he would not hit me but others would most likely suffer in my stead.

Even though we had already done everything sexually that we were going to do, my Mom denied me the satisfaction and comfort to sleep with the one I made love with. I agreed that was a right reserved for married people. Mom would call up and ask for me. She didn't know any of Volpes personally so I don't know how she got the phone number, but she did. She'd call and say, "Phillip, you need to come home tonight so you can go to church in the morning." That line got me every time. I haven't been to church on Sunday since I became a semi-retired Catholic - only going to church for special occasions. So if Anthony was too drunk or too mean we would walk home from Castleton no matter what time it was. We got it down pretty good. We would walk down Swarts Street and across Highland Avenue. Then we would walk fast for two blocks until we passed Queens Village. I was not a punk and had my natural strut to keep the weak ones away and figured if anyone stopped us I would say, "Have you seen our Uncle "Sammy V?" He told us to meet him somewhere around here."

When we got to Township Line Road, we were past the Castleton city limits. There were some houses and then about two hundred yards of undeveloped lots owned by the refinery and a cemetery we had to pass. People who lived in that area went to Manchester High School and we figured we would know them. Even though we were close to home, on a dark, lonely thoroughfare at that time of night you always had to look out when cars would pass. One night when an approaching car light shined on us, I'd said to Marie, "Tuck your hair in your shirt and start walking like a guy, if they think it's two guys, maybe we won't get jumped." She started calling me a pussy and saying she was not walking like a guy. And then she would say, "How do you want me to walk, like this?" Next, she proceeded to do exaggerated man strides. I said, "No, like this." And I started to walk like a gorilla. This distracted me enough to ease the tension and by then the car had passed. Soon we were back to our neighborhood in Driftwood. It was risky because you didn't want to seem drunk or silly or show any kind of weakness; some people see that as a green light to get you. We were lucky those nights that we didn't run across some real predators. ∽

# Chapter 11: Bad Rhythm

In early September of 1971, Marie's father made her quit school and work with him in his new pizza shop in the East End of Castleton. The clientele were mostly factory workers stopping in for lunch and the old man needed her to help out in the day. I felt bad for her. She wasn't a good student and I know she hated all the trouble caused by her brothers with the teachers and other students. But to quit school at sixteen was too young. As far as the old man was concerned, all a person needed was an eighth-grade education to get by. Who gave a shit about World History or Geography, Biology, or another language? He knew another language, but all I remember him saying every time he would get mad at the boys was "Mangiare visa tua mama!" I heard it a lot from him and I was sickened when I found out that it meant: "Go eat out your mother."

I would go to school and poor Marie would work for the old man. Her brother, Samuel worked with them. He was my age and had already quit school and was married with two kids by the time he was seventeen. Marie's only pay was that she got to keep the tip money from the customers. She would come home and after she made dinner for the family, we would use her tips to go down to Romeo's and play pinball and smoke cigarettes. I didn't have an official curfew. I just needed to be home before my mom went to work at night. Mom always wants every one of her kids still in school to be in the house and safe before she went to work. Marie's old man's enterprise didn't last long, just like the other three shops he had. They failed mainly because he was always too generous with the amount of toppings he put on his pizzas and, Marie told me that her brothers would rob him blind by taking money out of the cash register. After the shop went out of business, Marie would have to stay at home and clean the house and wash clothes all morning and cook supper for everyone before she could go out with me. One day while I was sitting in the kitchen waiting for Marie to finish the dishes, I heard someone say; "You fucking cunt, you. You better get in there before I cut you in half; you fucking no good cunt bastard, you." More curious than afraid, I looked into the living room and saw it was her fourteen-year-old brother, Angelo, trying to re-lace his sneakers.

After a month or so, Marie got another job. This time it was at a luggage factory out in Lennox Township just on the other side of Upper Manchester. Someone heard they were hiring assembly line workers. Marie and her neighbor, Bunny, applied for a job. They were hired on the spot and began work the next day. She would tell me how bad the smell was from the glue she used to seal the luggage parts together. She liked working with her friend and, since Bunny had her own car, they would drive to work together. Marie was only making minimum wage, but for an eighth-grade dropout, that was better than working for the old man.

She was only working at the luggage factory for about two weeks when Marie called me as soon as I walked in the front door to my house after school. She usually had her timing down so I could at least change clothes and grab a bite to eat. This was different I could tell right away something was very wrong.

In a crying voice, she said, "Phillip I have something bad to tell you."

I said, "What is it, Marie?"

She said, "I did something wrong and I'm sorry. I couldn't help myself."

She started to cry harder.

I said, "What, did you do cheat on me?"

"No, I would never cheat on you, ever. Please help me, Phillip."

I said, "Where are you now?"

She said, "I'm at a payphone by Wilsons' Drug store."

I said, "Is anyone with you?"

She said, "No, I'm by myself. I don't want anyone to know."

I said, "Anyone to know what?"

She didn't answer.

I said, "Stay there and I'll come to you."

I hung up the phone and hurried out the door of my house to go meet her. Wilsons' was only two blocks from my house. I ran most of the way and when I slowed down I was thinking what the hell have I got myself into? How was I going to handle this? Marie never cries so this must be bad.

As she saw me, she just hugged me and broke down sobbing saying, "I saw it. I saw it. I'm so sorry. It just came out."

I asked, "What came out Marie?"

"The baby did. I had a miscarriage at work today."

I asked, "Are you sure?"

She said, "Yes!"

She began to cry louder, Marie gave me a despondent look that said, "Don't give me a hard time right now. Just listen to me for a second."

It was a tiny curled up little baby. I could even see its eyes. It was all a big mess of blood and water. I flushed it down the toilet."

She just burst into tears. "I'm sorry for doing this to you."

I said, "Don't worry and don't be sorry for me. Tell me how this could have happened?"

She said, "I was at work and I felt sick and I had a lot of pressure down there, motioning to her lower abdomen, so I walked to the bathroom and when I sat on the toilet it just came out with all this blood."

Marie looked bad. All that I wanted to do is make sure she was taken care of. We walked around a little bit just talking about what to do. I wanted her to tell her mother.

She said, "No, she will tell my father and he will kill me."

I asked, "Do you want me to tell my mother?"

She said, "No she will hate me for the rest of my life."

I said, "No she won't, she is a nurse and she knows about this stuff."

I suggested we go to a doctor on Manchester Avenue. She did not want to because he was too close to home. I could see that even though Marie changed out of her work clothes and put on two Kotex napkins, the blood was showing out the back. I took off my jacket and put it around her waist. She looked pale and was starting to get weak from walking. We sat on the three-foot-high cinder block wall lining the Youth Center.

I said, "Marie, please, you have to tell your mother."

After a long wait, she finally decided to tell her mother. Mrs. Volpe gave her twenty dollars and told her to go to the doctor down in Penn's Port. We knew of him because people used to go to him for diet pills. We walked down to Penn's Port to see Doctor Mallard. I don't think he was a real doctor. After an hour's wait, he gave Marie an examination and some pills and told her to go home and go to bed. We walked back up to Driftwood. She went inside of her house and I went home not telling a soul about what happened.

The next day I went to school as if nothing ever happened. When I got home and just as I walked in the door the phone rang. It was Marie calling to tell me she was in the hospital.

"Excuse me, where are you?"

"I'm in Sacred Heart Hospital. Last night I got up to go to the bathroom and I passed out. The next thing I know I'm in the hospital getting a D and C."

"What the hell is a D and C?" I asked.

"It's when they scrape your insides out."

"Are you all right now?"

She said, "Yes."

I asked," Can I come up to see you?"

She said, "Yes, visiting hours are at 8 p.m."

I said, "I don't want anyone from my family to know anything about this. Do you think your parents can give me a ride?"

Marie said she would ask. Believe it or not, they gave me a ride and neither of them ever said a word to me, except her mom said, "If anyone asked, tell them Marie had a cyst on her ovary and it had to be removed."

I can't believe I had the nerve to get in the car with the old man, but I did. Marie looked fine, still pale but her face had signs of relief. In those days you could still smoke cigarettes in the hospital and she asked me for one. I looked at the old man first because she never smoked in front of him before. I remembered the time Marie told me the story of when he caught her smoking at age twelve; he made her eat a pack of cigarettes. She asked if it was alright and he said, "Yea."

When I returned home from seeing Marie my Mom stopped me as I was passing by my parent's bedroom.

My Dad was in there with her when she said, "Phillip, I want to talk to you."

I knew mom knew something but I wasn't going to tell her about Marie's condition. After all, it was my fault Marie was in this condition as much as it was hers.

"What happened to Marie last night?" my mom asked.

I said, "Nothing that I know of." I never was a good liar.

She asked, "Is she in the hospital?"

I replied, "Yes."

"Why is she in there?"

I said," She is having a cyst removed from her ovaries."

"Phillip, I work with the doctor that treated her and he told me that she had a miscarriage."

I knew that doctors couldn't tell what patients were in the hospital for. I thought it was probably one of those rat fink ambulance drivers from Driftwood firehouse that told my parents.

I said, "If that's what happened, no one told me." I hated to lie, but I could not tell my parents the truth. If Marie was willing to bleed to death to keep it a secret, who was I to tell someone, even if it was my mother. I think my mom knew what I was going through and didn't ask me any more questions. Besides, I think my mom told the doctor story just to get me to admit what happened. I never told anyone what happened until now. My mother gave me my heart and soul and I was slowly but surely giving it away to Marie.

Marie came home after three days in the hospital and we spent a lot of time together. We didn't talk about what happened very much. Marie recovered quickly. Her parents approved the doctor's recommendation that she start taking the birth control pill. I didn't give it much thought and accepted this as a sign of the times. After a few weeks, we went right back to our old ways. She always acted mature and confident and I liked that about her. The next time we tried to have sex was the first and only time I had trouble getting an erection. Usually, as soon as I stood still and knew we were going to do it, effectus erectus was standing tall. Not this time, I could not at first, but we were persistent and after a couple of tries and a change of location (to behind another bush), we were at it again. Much later, there were times when we were alone together and the subject would come up and she would say; "Phillip you should have seen it, it looked like a lost soul. It had really tiny fingers and little black dots for eyes. I feel so bad for it." And then, she would say, "My mom says it was the best thing that could have happened." My mom never said anything to me about it. But I know it really bothered her.

From the very beginning of our relationship, Marie was jealous as hell. She went through three blue star sapphire rings. She got mad for some reason and threw the first ring down the sink. Another one ended up in Sun Oil property because she tossed it over the fence. I would usually wait a week or two and replace it for her. I could not stand it. In the winter, we spent a lot of time in her parents' house. I couldn't even watch television with her. "Oh, you like watching those Farrah Fawcett commercials, don't you?"

"No, I don't," I'd say. When the Sound of Music came on she was jealous of Julie Andrews. I never understood that part of her. If she was watching her favorite soap opera, All My Children, because of the good-looking guys, I didn't care as long as she didn't pucker her lips as the TV characters were about to kiss. Occasionally, her jealously subsided, but it would resurface every now and again. I didn't think of it until later, but I should have told her how ugly being jealous made her. Because, when I finally did say that, it put a damper on her jealous comments, at least for a while.

Jimmy, my oldest brother, was getting out of the Air Force and he asked me if I wanted to go down to South Carolina with him during his last three days of active duty. I said, "Sure why not?" Marie and I were spending a lot of time together and we needed a break from each other. I told Marie that I was going with Jimmy and she was sad, but I didn't think much of it. What could a few days mean to a couple like us?

We drove down in Jim's yellow Volkswagen Beetle. This was the first time I was leaving the tri-state area without a parent or grandparent. Jim was cool and we almost always got along. He didn't like that I smoked cigarettes. He'd give me a hard time about it, so I just stopped smoking around him. It was odd when I asked him whose cigarettes were up in the sun visor of his car. He said they were his girlfriend's. On the way down to his Air Force Base, he kept telling me about this barmaid's daughter named Daniela. He kept saying how attractive she was and that she was my age and how all the airmen liked her. I guessed he really liked her. We made it down to the base that night and went to see a friend of his that lived with his wife in a trailer park. I got to meet the sergeant and his wife and they were nice people.

After dinner, Jim and I went to the base. I was surprised that I didn't have a hard time getting past security at the front gate. I guess a lot had to do with the fact that Jim was a Buck Sergeant and had a base sticker for his car and military ID, and I only had a dumb look on my face. We didn't have a problem getting to the barracks either. I met one of James' roommates. He was from the Boston area. James and he got along fine. The guy whose bunk I slept in was a Black airman. When I asked if he needed his bed that night, they said he preferred to stay in a room with the other Black guys. That night I had to have a smoke, so I reluctantly got out of my bunk very quietly and went outside. I met an Airman who asked who I was. I told him I was with my brother, James Webster. Luckily he knew and was friendly with him. I asked him for a smoke and he gave me one. That was the best smoke I had in a while but it made me realize that I was hooked on them. The next day we went to the mess hall. I was a little afraid to get in line with the other guys so I just went to the orange juice fountain and got a drink. James got something light to eat before he went to an administration building so he could do paperwork and I waited outside. I was dying for a cigarette. I stole one of his girlfriend's and I smoked it. His girlfriend just happened to leave some matches too.

We went to pick up Jim's friend and his wife, so we could go to the local lake to picnic and swim. James kept saying how he hoped that Daniela would be there. I really didn't care. As it turned out she was not there. I walked around the picnic area staying away from the water because I wasn't getting anywhere near that snake-infested lake. Later that night we all went to a bar the Airmen frequented. Our party consisted of the sergeant and his wife, James and his friend from Boston, and me. The bar was the same one that Daniela's mother worked. I guess it was typical. It had a pebble covered dirt parking lot. The insides were dank with sawdust on the wooden floor and plenty of beer advertising around. It smelled of stale beer and cigarettes. By now Jim was told that Daniela would not be there because she was visiting her father in Georgia. I really didn't care if she was there or not.

I was a little anxious about going inside with a bar full of loud drunk people because I was only eighteen years old and had never been in a bar before. I didn't know what the legal age for drinking beer was in this state but I figured I'd be alright because I was with my big brother. We all went inside and Jim and his friends bought me beer. The bar had three pool tables and an amusement game where you slid this metal disc down a wooden table to slide over these triggers that pushed bowling pins up and out of the way. Over in the corner of the room was a big old jukebox blaring country and western music. We all took turns playing pool. The sergeant was very good at pool. He played for money against these other guys in the bar.

The next thing I know James says, "Quick! Get out of here, there is going to be a fight." The sergeant won and one of the guys that lost was very upset. I was handing my pool stick to James when this short little punk takes a full swing with his pool stick at my head. James was facing him and saw this coming, so he took my stick and blocked it and broke the punk's pool stick. At the same time I put up my arm up to defend myself but the fat end of the punks stick swung around my arm and hit me on the side of my head just above my left ear. I stumbled backward and hit the slide-bowling table. I felt myself sliding down to the floor. My peripheral vision was turning black and was closing in on the center. I was just about to pass out when suddenly it reversed and I recovered. I was able to collect my thoughts. I saw Jim was fighting another guy. The guy that hit me ran back to his friends when he realized he only had a small stick left and James was standing there with a full stick in his hands. The next thing I saw was my brother with his back against the jukebox defending himself against one of the punk's friend's punches while the initial aggressor was trying to throw pool balls at my brother. The guy couldn't get a clear shot at James because his partners were in the way. Just then, I grabbed the metal disk used to slide down the table and throw it at the guy. I had this guy in my sights. I had tunnel vision. He was all mine. But I couldn't pull the trigger. I knew if I threw it, I might kill him. The next thing I knew the bar bouncer was in the middle of the bar carrying a nightstick trying to stop the fight; simultaneously the barmaid was yelling that she called the police and they were on the way. As I went outside, I could see the friends of the guy that hit me telling him to take off before the cops came. He hopped on his motorcycle and rode away. I could have hit him in the head with a rock as he was riding away but I didn't take the chance. That night I had a really bad headache and my brother asked if I wanted to go to the hospital, but I told him, no. The next day Jim finished his discharge paperwork and we drove home.

The ride back up to Pennsylvania was uneventful. My headache was subsiding and James played his Grand Funk Railroad greatest hits tape all the way home. As soon as we arrived home, I went to see Marie. Before I made it to her house, a couple of her brothers and some of their friends were in the playground.

That Black guy I boxed under the bridge said, "Boy, I don't know what you did to that girl, because all she did for the past two days was sit on the front porch rocking on her chair staring out at the refinery."

Before I could reach the front yard her little sister ran up to Marie and told her I was coming. Marie pretended as if she didn't care but we both knew that we didn't like being apart for very long. For the next two hours, we just sat there listening to Elton John's -Tumble Weed Connection. ✑

## Chapter 12: Skank Writing All Over Me

Hanging around the Volpes was all right. I never went over there without Marie calling me first. I called her a few times, but if she didn't answer the phone, no one else did. I was at their house when the phone rang. Her brothers sitting close to the phone ignored it. But Marie always answered the phone and normally, before she did, those nearby would say, something like, "If it's for me, tell them I'm not here," or "See who it is and take a message."

In our house, common courtesy said if you're the closest to the phone when it rang, you answered it. It paid off for me once. El Dorado Pete was out in California trying to get a movie made about some jewel thief he knew. He met and told a Hollywood actor best known at this time for his starring role in a Wild West TV show about his movie plan. Pete told him about his girlfriend's good looks. After hearing this, the TV actor wanted to invite my sister Ann out to California for a screen test. Well, I answered the phone and Petie asked to talk to Ann so I ran upstairs to get her. She said, "Go tell him I'll be down to talk in a minute." Well, Pete put the actor on the phone, I guess to impress my sister with his celebrity and to try and convince Ann to come out to California. Instead, he got me telling him that Ann will be down in a minute. Ann never went out to California. When I asked why she said that she didn't have the right clothes or makeup to wear.

While hanging out at Marie's house, there were plenty of things to do. Her younger siblings were there all the time and they were brats. They took pleasure in bothering me. I could always feel this uneasy tension in the air. Early in our relationship, her mother said to me, "Don't you think you two are too young to be going steady?"

I just said, "I don't know."

The fact that Marie's old lady was married and had a child at the age of fifteen may have had something to do with her worries and of course Marie's miscarriage didn't help either.

When I was working at the diner washing dishes I made a dollar an hour. I made just enough pocket change to get by. Marie's brothers and I used to spend a lot of time playing cards and bull shitting the evening away. We would play poker and twenty-one blackjack. Mostly, it was Fredrico, Popeye, Samuel and me. Samuel would keep things interesting by asking questions like, "Do farts make queers horny?" And Popeye would sit and mumble under his breath unintelligible comments that only Fredrico seemed to comprehend and sometimes, in turn, Fredrico would make comments like, "Sure, if you say so." Well, the card games we were playing were only for quarters, but somehow I would lose money every time, even after I changed my seat from directly in front of the glass knick-knack closet. And to think they probably made Marie clean the glass right before we started playing cards so the glass would reflect the cards I was holding in my hand. After I lost about three dollars, one of them would go out and buy cigarettes and beer on my money. Well, I got tired of it. I bought my own deck of cards and marked them. I left the aces and face cards alone. I marked 2-3-4 one-way and the 5-6-7 another and the 8-9 yet another way. While playing 21 blackjack, I knew within three numbers of what the next card was and it didn't help me. I still lost. If I needed a 10 or face card it would be a 5, 6, or 7. I retired from playing cards for money after that.

In the late summer of 1971, I was still hanging around with my friends Timmy, Gunther, and Dave but most of the time I was at the Volpe's house. Around this time Marie's brother Fredrico decided to join the Air Force. There were a few hurdles he needed to overcome before he could enlist. He had outstanding fines and other legal business in his past that he needed to clear before he could join in Pennsylvania. Someone told him that he did not have to join from Pennsylvania instead he could join from another state and they would not have his records. They told him to go and enlist in Newark, Delaware. He liked this idea and asked me if I would ride down to Newark with him. I said sure, why not. I asked Fredrico why he wanted me to go with him and he said, "I don't want to go down to Newark alone because of all the riots that took place there." I told him that the riots were in Newark, New Jersey and not Newark, Delaware. It was at that time I wondered if he really didn't know the difference between the two states or if he was just telling me anything that came to his mind because he did not want to tell me the real reason and, perhaps he thought I didn't know the difference. I always felt as if Fredrico was a pathological liar. I do believe that some people living in the inner city around this time didn't need to go outside of their own neighborhood for anything. For a lot of people, their whole world was within a five-mile radius. Anything outside of that area was as if it were a foreign land. Marie said she was never outside of Castleton until she moved to Driftwood. She said when she was younger she thought the state of California was something the television people made up. It only existed as a backdrop for actors and cameramen. It is true that the news stations constantly reported on some of the wild and crazy things coming from California. In the 1960s and early 1970s, if it wasn't the stories of the Hells Angels Motor Cycle Gang hurting concertgoers at a Rolling Stones concert or the Black Panthers Party being militant, it was Charles Manson doing his thing. It didn't help California's reputation when Senator Robert F. Kennedy was assassinated either. As far as I was concerned the whole world was acting crazy and California was its Mecca.

I ended up having an uneventful trip down to Newark, Delaware with Fredrico as he signed himself up for the US Air Force.

That same year my brother Gerald joined the Air Force. Mom's stomach still bothered her but she remained at her job. Dad seemed all right. He did a lot around the house but still didn't have a paying job. My maternal grandmother, Nana was still with us getting around the house with her cane. Elizabeth was still a nun teaching grade school around Baltimore. Ann and Holly stayed with us; Ann still dating El Dorado Pete. Katherine continued to work and help out with the bills. James returned home from military service, stopped getting his hair cut and a few months after that he announced that he was moving out of the house. I don't know if it was our mother's maternal feelings or financial but I could tell she didn't like the fact James was leaving home. She was 'blue' all the time. John stayed home and worked at Sun Rock Manufacturing Co. where they made water fountains. I quit my job washing dishes at the diner when my boss accused me of giving food to a friend. I didn't do this and it angered me that he would accuse me with no real evidence. I wasn't going to work for someone that unjust. With the addition of John helping with the family's finances, my mom was able to send my younger sisters Mary and Joan to a Catholic high school in Delaware. Kevin, Ruth, and Holly were still at Holy Sacrament.

Both my brother Gerald and Marie's brother Fredrico were in the Air Force. Like our oldest brother James, Gerald's first overseas duty was in South Korea, and later he was stationed in Thailand. Fredrico was already in Thailand. The war was still going on in Vietnam and if I had to go into the military, that's how I would like it, at least one country (Cambodia) between me and the combat. But that was not the case for a lot of GIs. They had to face the challenge given to them by the communist and our country's leaders. I was turning 18 years old that September and President Nixon was seeking a second term as president campaigning on a promise to end the war with honor.

The television stations continued to show war footage and college students protesting it. I didn't mind the students so much, but the thing I don't remember is if the time the college students started to demonstrate was after they lost their draft deferments. The television news showed some of the French demonstrating outside the Paris Peace Talks and that upset me. I didn't appreciate these foreigners saying bad things about us. They had their chance and lost it and now we were there trying to fix their mistakes. In March 1971 the U.S. government lowered the voting age from twenty-one to eighteen. This change came about peacefully when the civilians argued if an 18-year-old can go to fight and die in the war, then they should be allowed to vote for the people that set the laws to send them there. At this time I still believed that even though we were in a war that caused massive heartache we could win the war and keep the communist out of South Viet Nam. Our enemies, the communists, were certainly going to continue to punish or kill everyone under their control that disagreed with them. As far as I was concerned the choices between communism and capitalism were already decided. After World War II, Viet Nam gained its independence from France and it was agreed that the Communists would live up North and govern the people their way and the Capitalists would do the same in the south. The most glaring examples to me as to which 'way of life' is best were in North and South Korea, East and West Germany, Main Land and Taiwan, China.

September 1971 I started my senior year at Manchester Senior High School and my friend Gunther Price quit school and joined the Army. He was going to report for Basic Training at Fort Dix, New Jersey the next day. Gunther, Danny DeMarco and I were looking for something to do that night so we decided to break into the local Union Hall. There was already a way to get through the back fence and onto the property. Marie and I used this opening several times when we wanted to be alone.

Danny, Gunther, and I slipped through the fence and broke into the building through the back door. The main room had a podium, gavel, bench, and a judge's chair. We pretended as if we were in a court of law. We used Danny as the defendant. I was the judge and Gunther was the defense attorney. I would say, "This little pervert needs to get locked up before he procreates." Gunther said, "He's too lazy to be a pro at anything." Danny just said, "Fuck you, you are both assholes." After that comment, he was in contempt and definitely had to be locked up. Just clowning around, we grabbed him and went to lock him up in the back room. As we opened the door we found a safe. It was a 3ft. X 3ft. metal box with a combination locked door in the front. It looked too inviting to leave alone. Gunther and I decide to take the safe out the back door so we could open it later. Danny had had enough mischief for a school night and went home. The safe was heavy but we got it out the back door. We tumbled it down the back four concrete steps and pushed it next to the fence near the hole we crawled through. We pulled on the fence to stretch and enlarge the hole so we could force the safe through. We got it through the fence and into Driftwood Elementary School's playground and set it next to a tree. This wasn't going to do even for a temporary hiding place. I saw Marie's younger brother Carlo and asked him to let us use the old man's wheelbarrow, so we could move the safe. He loaned it to us, and we moved the safe across the playground and hid it in some bushes in the back yard of the Volpe's next-door neighbor. Gunther went to the DeMarco's to stay the night and I went home so I could go to school the next day. I went to my first two periods and decided to walk out the back door of the school to met Gunther in Driftwood. My brother John was laid off of work so he was home. I asked him if he would help us move the safe to the woods behind Mickey Vernon Little League baseball fields. He agreed and the three of us used his car to go and pick up the safe. The playground was surrounded by the school and its parking lot adjacent to the post office on the south side, four homes including the Volpes to the east, Driftwood police station, the Youth Center, the union hall to the north and some more homes to the west, all facing away from the playground. We could see the police out in front of the union hall investigating the break-in while we were loading the safe in the back of John's red 1963 Chevy Impala convertible. As Gunther and I were lifting the heavy object into the trunk, the owner of the house came out and started to holler at us. "What the hell are you guys doing in my yard?" We barely had enough strength to pick the safe high enough to get it in the trunk. With the last heave-ho, we succeeded in placing the safe into John's car trunk. But the safe was too big and it wouldn't allow us to close the trunk door. So we left it open.

Gunther and I jumped in the car without opening the door. Just as John started to take off the school's recess bell rang and about fifty kids started running out of the school towards the playground. It seemed as if each and every child was yelling and screaming, trying to be the first one to the swings. We sped out of there like nobody's business all the while the trunk door bounced on the safe. My brother John was getting into it. He was yelling, "Kiss my ass, you old bastard," as his tires shot grass and dirt at the old man. Gunther was trying to reach out the back seat to keep the trunk door from causing too much of a scene. As it turned out, we escaped out of there without a problem.

When we made it to our predetermined wooded area less than a few blocks away, John backed his car up to the edge of the woods and Gunther and I lifted the safe out of the car. As John drove away, we rolled it down a path. We weren't exactly sure where we were going to settle our new treasure until we noticed a small clearing just off the path and out of sight from anyone traveling along the road. We tried to open it with only a flat screwdriver and hammer to see what was inside, but failed and gave up when Gunther had to go catch his ride to Boot Camp at Fort Dix, New Jersey.

The next couple of days I would go there by myself. The word spread about what we did and guys from the neighborhood started to ask what was inside. Carlo wanted his cut for letting us use the wheelbarrow. I did not tell anyone where we hid the safe but I did tell Carlo I would let him know when I opened it. I wasn't in a hurry because I really didn't care what I would find. I took Marie up there a couple of times but after working on it for about ten minutes we would stop to have sex. Neither Marie nor I cared about material things. Getting into the safe wasn't easy as it had an outside shell of 1/16 of an inch of steel plate. This covered a 1-inch layer of concrete with wire mesh reinforcement. Another 1/16 inch of steel plate formed the inner box that held the contents. All in all, it took me about two weeks to get inside using a claw hammer and screwdriver. I did this by starting to chisel on a seam and worked my way through. When I finally got to the contents all I found were canceled checks, someone from Delaware's Will and Testament and the deed to the Union Hall. The next day on my way over to the other side of Driftwood I dropped the deed and the Will in a US Post Office mailbox.

A little more than a month later, Marie and I were misbehaving just like we did every chance we got. That evening we left the dance soon after it started at about 7:30 p.m. just when the sun was going down. We walked down to the Hewes Avenue Park. The park at that time was an undeveloped lot with a footpath to the baseball fields. I had four or five beers earlier and I was really drunk. Marie drank her usual bottle of wine and she was feeling wild too. We walked into the park just far enough to where the weeds were knee-high. That's all we needed. We dropped down and I used my long neck to do my impression of a prairie dog lifting my head up to look around for predators. I wanted to see if the coast was clear. It was clear, so we got down to business. I don't remember a lot, but we did things no Catholic boy or girl should ever admit to doing. We tasted the forbidden fruit. After that episode, the number sixty-nine had a flavor and sensation all of its own. Following our unbiblical deeds, we fell asleep in the park and, as soon as we woke up, I walked Marie home and went home myself.

Early the next morning I was awakened by my youngest sister, Ruth. I felt sick and was covered with a rash from head to toe. I thought, oh shit! Marie and I must have been fooling around in a patch of poison ivy. It was instant karma. I was brought back into the moment by Ruth saying, "Someone is at the door for you." I thought, "Damm it; I'm in trouble again." Not in trouble, instead it was Gunther Price home from Boot Camp and wanting to see me. He was curious about what was in the safe. He wanted me to ride around town and hang out with him. I told him nothing of value to us was in there but he wanted to hear more. In spite of feeling ill, scratching my sores until they bled, and having "I'm a skank" written all over my body, I went and spent the day visiting all of our friends and trying to avoid explaining how I got poison ivy all over my body. Later that night when I finally got away to meet Marie, she was not allowed out. Her sister told me that she was worse than I was and needed to go to the doctor to get a shot of medicine. Oh well! I never said I was smart. ৩

# Chapter 13: Just a Clue

My senior year in high school was coming to an end and I really didn't give a shit if I graduated or not. No one I knew ever got a job at Sun Oil or B.P refineries. And only the first two females in my family went to college. My third oldest sister Katherine was definitely smart enough but did not attend college. I am sure she felt getting a steady paying job at the hospital was the immediate solution to our family's money problems. The males I admired most spent their first summer after high school hanging around Driftwood and in September joined the military. My mother insisted that I graduate, so I stayed to make up my credits and completed the last semester. I had fun when I took Marie to my senior prom. I didn't have a car so her brother Matthew and his girlfriend Virginia drove us up to the event held at the prestigious, Downing Town Inn. We enjoyed the dinner and dancing. I'm glad I went and I'm glad Marie was able to go with me. Marie was a little embarrassed by the fact she had to borrow a dress from my sister Katherine. In spite of that, I know Marie was glad she went with me.

The early summer was calm, but I did learn a little tidbit about her old man. One warm Friday Matthew, Popeye, Samuel, and I were helping the old man repair the roof of their house. We did this by tearing off old shingles and plywood and replacing them with new ones. Things seemed normal until evening approached and Matthew said, "I got to go. I have a date with Virginia." Five minutes later Samuel said, "I needed to go and see Patty, his estranged wife, and the kids." That's when the old man turned and said to Popeye, "How about you?" Popeye said nothing. The old man said, "When I was your age, if I didn't have a piece of ass every night, God help the first faggot I ran into."

Well, there's something to be said about, "like father, like son." I say that because of something Samuel said to me one afternoon when I was complaining about the hot weather. I said, "It's got to be a hundred fucking degrees out here today." Samuel replied, "No shit, today would be a good day to be in jail."

I said, "Excuse me? Did you just say, today would be a good day to be in Jail?" He said, "Yea, with all that steel and concrete it's always cool in there."

Samuel was only eighteen but he had already been locked up a few times for petty crimes. He never stayed locked up too long because he was married and had two kids and someone would always bail him out.

I said to him, "Yea, but isn't it a pain in the ass to be stuck in jail with all the horny White trash and niggers."

His reply was, "Well, you won't have any problem shitting after that." End of conversation.

Late summer of 1972, with the help of Anthony's wife Judy, I got a job in Castleton as a receiving inspector at a place called Precision Products. They made small parts for military tanks. My job was to make sure the components we received met the specifications on the purchase order. It was easy enough. I had my mother's work ethic and was getting smarter as I matured.

The next month I received my draft notice. It stated that on November 23rd I had to report to Delaware County Court House in Media, Pennsylvania. The day I received my draft notice I told Marie that, if I got drafted and had to go into the army, we should break up and, that she was not obligated to wait for me. She seemed bothered by this. I'm not sure if she understood exactly what I meant. What I meant was, for each new day, we would choose for that day and only that day to wait to be together. She and I both knew there was a slight chance that I might have to go to Vietnam.

Even though the United States was de-escalating the war in Vietnam, the selective service center continued to have a lottery drawn every year with a number coinciding with your birth date. In 1972, my number was seventy. Marie's brother Samuel had a draft number of fifty-five. I had already decided not to join any military service; I felt as if I had no business in any of them. I could not understand why, if all Christians followed the teachings of Jesus Christ, was it all right to kill another human being? I knew that "eye for an eye" and all the Old Testament stuff was okay for the Jews and Muslims and because of that, their wars would last till the end of time, but I couldn't figure out how we Christians could get past all the "turn the other cheek" and "do unto others" teachings from Jesus. Isn't that why everyone with any sense of what was going on admired Dr. Martin Luther King? I know I did.

Being a Catholic, I noticed when the television showed news clips from the combat zones, the priest would get together with the troops and hold a Mass out in the field. This confused me and I was going to have to see a priest about it if I ever got drafted. I wanted to live a guilt-free life. Even though I thought that the Catholic clergy took themselves too seriously, I counted on the priest to tell me what was going to get me into heaven or, more importantly, how to stay out of hell. Trying to understand religion baffled me so, whenever I read the Bible on my own, I would have to stop and think about what it really meant for a week.

I did know, as working-class Americans, we didn't like bullies and that bullies only go as far as the subject of their attention lets them. And the communists were world-class bullies. We were okay with unions but not commies. I feared going over there and being told to kill some poor peasant by some gung-ho officer or some sergeant because they wanted some revenge for something that happened for no good reason. I couldn't blame a person for wanting to kill me for coming to his country with a gun in my hand to tell him how to live his life. I didn't care that the French lost in the earlier war. They were there as colonialists and I didn't want to be any part of that. I was going to allow myself to be drafted because I was an American citizen and my country needed me. It was a very confusing time for me.

In November, when my date for the physical arrived, my dad and I drove over to the Volpe's to pick up Samuel. We rode to Media to get on the buses with about a hundred and twenty-five other poor suckers in the same mess as we were in. The buses dropped us off at the Induction Center on Broad Street in Philadelphia. First, we all stood in line to hand in our letters and get checked in. Then some army corporal took about thirty of us in a room and issued a written test. I disliked tests, but this one started out easy. The written exam remained this way for about the first ten questions. When I take tests in a group, I am always aware of the time limit and who finished first. That person usually slapped their pencil down hard enough so everyone else taking the test knew that they were the first ones done. Then, the next one finished did the same, and so on, until even the test givers started talking to them while they waited for me to finish my test. Well, the same thing happened here. I was so stupid. I tried to do well and became competitive when I heard this distinctive sound. I knew exactly what it was. It was Samuel sucking his front teeth. He would push his tongue against the inside of his upper two front teeth and suck air and saliva through the gap caused by his cavities. He did this when he was acting cool, as in when we played cards and he was sitting with a good hand and he just sat there waiting for me to ante up some more money. Sure enough, I turned around and I saw him leaning back looking around like he was on top of the world. He was finished way before me. The questions kept getting harder until they changed subjects. They had these illustrated boxes that you had to turn around in your head to match the other boxes and all kinds of stuff I haven't seen before. Meanwhile, I kept trying to figure out how the hell did Samuel, an eighth-grade dropout, get smarter than me.

After our boxed lunch was the physical examination. That's where you had to take off everything except your tee shirt and underpants. I always wore tighty-whities and never wore an undershirt. I was hanging around with Samuel and a couple of other guys and we started to loosen up by saying humorous stuff just to lighten up the situation. I sensed we were all nervous about the entire situation, especially the grand finale when you have to drop them, turn, and cough and then turn around, bend over, and spread them. We all had to know that this was coming and it weighed heavily on my mind. We got our height and weight recorded and gave a vial of blood. I was six feet and one hundred and fifty-five pounds. We walked towards the lavatories and the attendant gave me a cup and said, "Put your specimen in this." I said, "Do you want me to fill it up with a number one or a number two." This humored a few guys around me but not the private giving me the cup. As it turned out, I was too nervous to pee. Sheepishly I had to ask the same private if I could come back and try again. The final scene was when about twenty of us stood in a line shoulder to shoulder, facing the doctor and he said, "Alright, drop 'em." Here we are, all standing there with our underpants down around our ankles. When I looked straight down at myself, I didn't feel very confident with what I saw. I couldn't help but look around and compare. I noticed that a few of them looked semi-erect. I tried to think of Marie so I could add some length and girth to give whoever looked at me a better show, but I had no luck. Then I remembered what Matthew Volpe told Samuel and me the night before. He said, "When the doctor sticks his finger around your asshole everyone there can see who the fags are. He who gets a boner is a faggot." As it was, I couldn't wait till the doctor checked my anus for piles, then I could pull up my underpants again. My ass I could match up with anyone, but my doddle, well it needed a little inspiration before I wanted anyone looking at it.

After that, they told us to go into a small room to talk to a doctor, one on one. I thought this was my chance to let them know my problems that a mass checkup wouldn't find. The doctor said, "Is there anything you feel as though I should know." I told him about the time I had a wet dream and how my hands would sweat all the time. I also said how I had heart compensation. He said, "What?" I said, "One night I woke up and my heart was beating really fast and then it would stop, and then start again."

He said, "What did you do?" I said, "I thought I was going to die, so I went downstairs to where my mom kept all the religious artifacts to get a scapular. I laid it on my chest because I knew if you died with a scapular on, you go immediately to heaven." He said, "Thank you. You may go now." I found out a couple of weeks later that he wasn't a regular MD but that he was a psychiatrist.

Two weeks later I got my acceptance letter saying I passed and I got a fifty-seven on the test and my status was 1-A. I was not to leave the area without notifying the local draft board. I heard Samuel got a seven and was excused because of his low score and the fact he had a wife and two kids. For the next month, the other services sent me letters asking me to join them because they saw my test scores and wanted men like me. But my mind was made up. Even if I got my call to report to basic training, I was not going to join any of them. Another letter came in December saying that the selective service was taking the first fifty numbers in the first quarter of 1973 and if they needed more they would select the next group to one hundred and twenty-five to reach their quota. I was in the second group. Lucky for me, Nixon ended the draft in 1973 and only a few guys were drafted. Nixon fulfilled a campaign promise and the Paris Peace Talks turned into the Paris Accords and we were able to continue our retreat from Vietnam.

In March of 1973, I wasn't sure what I was going to do with my life. I knew that I didn't want to stay in Driftwood. I couldn't get a good-paying job at the local refineries in spite of applying for a job every time the word spread that the refinery was hiring. If Marie and I wanted to have an undisturbed future together, this was not the time or place for us.

Marie was the true parent to her family. She fed them and cleaned their clothes and comforted them when they got sick or in trouble. One privilege Marie had was a bedroom of her own with a lock. She told me that her brothers asked her to keep some of their stuff locked in her room so others won't steal it. Her second oldest brother Salvadore asked her to keep his stash of marijuana in her room for safekeeping. I know it was hard for her to abstain from taking some of his pot, but she did. As time went by, we drank alcohol to get high less often. She asked me to sneak up to her room once, but I refused. Partly because if the old man caught me he would try to beat me up or I would get banned from coming in the house for life or at least of a couple of weeks until the old man cooled off. I don't think any of her brothers cared if we did sneak into her room except maybe Popeye, I bet he would have liked it, because, he would try to peek in on us. Marie told me that she never felt comfortable undressing in her room or taking a bath because she wondered if someone was spying on her. We didn't sneak into her room because I don't think it was right. Though, I thought it was okay to go outside or while babysitting because we never got paid by her brother for our services and I figured that having sex inside was our compensation. But never would we do it in either of our homes. When we were outside, we always thought that we were in our own little Eden. We only needed everyone else in the world to be preoccupied with something else before we acted upon our desires. Hell! There was this one time when it was really foggy in the middle of the day, as in you can't see your hand in front of your face. We did it standing upright in the middle of the playground about twenty feet from her back yard. Marie enjoyed doing stuff like that and to a certain extent so did I.

I figured that Marie had heavy issues with her parents. I remember one time early in our relationship, in a petting motion, I touched the back of her head. She stopped me and asked me not to do that. I insisted she tell me why. She said, "Okay, go ahead and feel it." When I did, through her very thick hair I felt a distinct flat spot on the back of her head. She told me that it was because her parents left her lying around a lot when she was firstborn. She continued to say, "They didn't want a girl and after I was born they never picked me up. I just laid there and my head grew in this position."

If that's the case or not, I don't know, but if she thinks it is, it's true enough for me. I wanted to cry for her, but I didn't.

My first year as a high school graduate was passing by. The draft was behind me and I was classified 1-H and I wanted a change. I was still working at Wire Pro in Castleton. My brother Jimmy was a welder at a nearby shipyard. On his way home he would swing by and give me a ride home. Once, while I was waiting for him to pick me up, a colored girl called me an "uppity White bastard." In retrospect, I should have known it was coming, I could hear her talking a block away. She had one of those voices that said, "I'm tired of people's bullshit and I am not going to take it anymore." I was standing in the middle of the sidewalk so I could see my brother's car coming and I took a step back as the girls approached walking three abreast. I could have taken another step back but didn't. This caused the loud mouth girl to walk around me and blurt the "White Bastard" line. I figured the call was fifty-fifty, part my fault, and part hers. In hindsight, I should have moved all the way out of their path. I don't know why I was holding my ground. Maybe, I *was* being uppity. After this, I realized I was in hostile territory, so I decided to wait inside until it was about time for James' arrival. But I also wanted to make it as easy as possible for James, so I would pop in and out of the factory every few minutes or so to see if he arrived.

A week later while waiting for James, two Black boys that looked about ten years old tried to rob me. They acted as if they did this a hundred times before. They didn't seem angry or afraid, just doing what was their inherent right to do. I don't think they were related to the girls, but these little hoods approached me without hesitation. The boys were standing side by side right in front of me. They said, "Give me all your money." At the same time that he spoke, he took a step back and put his hand inside his coat and down towards his waistline. He said, "I have a gun." He closed his mouth tight as if he wasn't going to say another word. I could tell he was bluffing so I looked at the other boy and he had this blank stare that said, "I'm with him." It was in late winter when they approached me. Both were wearing raggedy old clothes and had yellow snot running out of their nose. I could see it spilling out as he exhaled and retracted as he inhaled. Neither of the boys seems nervous at all. They were both suffering from one of those winter colds that lasted until spring, I could tell, and that if they would just be given some cold medicine, clean clothes, and plenty of rest it would clear up in a week or so. I was surprised and insulted by their actions. What did they think was going to happen? In this area of Castleton, I would expect a drug addict to do this, but in no way did I expect this from a couple of ten-year-old boys. The experience shocked me. I told them that I was a black belt in karate and that I was going to kick them across the street if they didn't leave. They both took a step back turned and walked away. I wanted to tell their mother on them but I didn't. I just wanted to get out of there.

Fredrico came home from Thailand and was now stationed at McGuire Air Force Base in New Jersey where he bought a new car. This allowed him to come home every weekend. It was a 1973 Chevy Malibu painted an ugly copper color but it had a nice clean new smell inside. He didn't care who drove it. At eighteen-years-old, I used it to take the driving test to get my driver's license. At that time, the car still had the proper tags from the dealer in New Jersey where he bought the car. Fredrico said he didn't have a driver's license, so I asked my brother John to go with me as I took the test. John was like that, you could ask him for any favor and he would do it. John didn't have any guy friends so I knew that I could treat him like a spare friend and he would come and help me if I needed a ride or something like that.

Around the same time, my sister Ann got pregnant by Petie. He wanted to marry her but she said, "No." She decided to go to Fort Lauderdale to have the baby. My brother Jimmy quit his job at the shipyard to take her down and stay with her until the baby was born. A few weeks later, Fredrico was reassigned to Homestead Air Force Base in southern Florida. I told Fredrico I wanted to ride down with him so I could go to Fort Lauderdale. He was happy to take me down so I could keep him company while he drove his car to the base. Marie didn't know what to think about the situation. I told her it was in our best interest and I would call her down when I got settled. I didn't see our relationship growing if we stayed there. She was the oldest daughter of a man that saw one reason for girls and that was to take care of the men in the family. Besides, there wasn't anywhere for us to grow in Driftwood and my job wasn't going to get any better than minimum wage. So I quit and went to Florida. ∽

# Chapter 14: Going South For the Winter

I felt sad when we left. Marie and I were sitting on her front porch staring at Sun Oil, waiting to say our goodbye. Fredrico came out of the house ready to go. Samuel came right behind him and said, "Be sure to bring me a monkey, when you come back." Samuel's request distracted me for a second but I wanted to tell Marie goodbye, I kissed her and said, "I'll see you soon." Then I proceeded to get into the car with Fredrico.

As we backed down their driveway, I could barely see Marie because of the awning and stuccoed wall around her front porch. She was sitting on her rocking chair and suddenly I began to lose my composure. My feelings began to rush from my heart to my stomach and lungs and then into my head, nose, and eyes. I had to fight back the tears. I didn't want her brother to see me become weak. So I just looked out the passenger side window away from Fredrico. I couldn't look at Marie any more. I looked down and I didn't wave bye when she came back into view as we pulled away. I also had a phobia about telling someone that I love them. I never said that to her, but I realized at that time, whether I wanted to or not, I did love her. I kept telling myself that this was the best move for us. And that the best chance for a bright future was away from Driftwood. If leaving her alone like this is what it would take, I was going to do it.

I was ready for this ride and I knew it took about twenty-four hours to drive from Driftwood to Fort Lauderdale. Once we were out of Delaware, I was no longer looking back but anxiously looking forward. Fredrico drove most of the way. At that time, Interstate 95 was incomplete and still under construction. This caused us to detour to within two hundred yards of the White House. I remember thinking if they only knew what kind of nuts were driving that close to the president's house. I mean some of the guys I knew would try to see if they could hit it with a rock. Once, her brother Angelo thought he could hit a commercial airliner on its landing approach to the Philadelphia Airport. No shit, this guy looked up and saw how big it looked and thought it was close enough to reach and started to throw rocks at it. Of course, this is the same guy who thought if you shot someone through the television screen during a live broadcast, you could kill him. Sincerely, we were standing in their living room one Saturday night watching a show called the Midnight Special. They showcased the latest entertainment mostly musical rock and roll bands. On this night, an acid rock band was playing. None of us liked long-haired guys, so we thought it was funny when Fredrico pulled out his gun and pretended to shoot the lead singer through the screen. When Angelo saw him, he said, "Don't shoot him, they will know it was us." We all just shook our heads. Marie's second oldest brother Sal went into a tirade ending with you got to be the dumbest mother-fucker ever born.

The trip went easy and money wasn't a problem because I cashed my last paycheck of eighty-five dollars and brought all of it with me. Fredrico had some money of his own so we could fill up the gas tank and get something to eat as we needed. Fredrico and I didn't talk about much. He was one of those people that stayed in the moment. We mostly talked about current events as in, are we still on the right road to Florida or, I didn't know North and South Carolina were two different states. I did ask him what Samuel meant about bringing him back a monkey. He said they were watching Mutual of Omaha's Wild Kingdom the other night. It was about wild monkeys in Central America's tropical jungles. Fredrico said when he told Samuel that south Florida is considered a semi-tropical region; Samuel must have put two and two together and figured that monkeys ran wild where we were going.

Fredrico is what some people refer to as a bullshit artist, he never tells the truth, not even on trivial things. I like to think of him as a lying sack of shit. This could have been caused by his family's business. I never asked questions about what his family did. I only knew that their Uncle Sammy worked with the organized criminals of Castleton. He was known as an enforcer. Their grandparents dealt with illegal "numbers" for the neighborhood. The "numbers racket" was a gambling game controlled by serious criminals. A person would pick a three-digit number and place a bet, the winning number is picked by the crime boss. The number was usually some combination of the number of the horse that won at a nearby racetrack. They were associated with the Italian and Black policy numbers racket. This was a nickel and dime game for inner-city residents. Uncle Sammy was also involved in other gambling activities and was one of the guys who came to collect the debt that you owed the boss.

The next morning we passed the Georgia state line and I wanted to get something to eat. Freddy didn't seem hungry, just anxious to get to where we were going. I saw a roadside billboard advertising fried chicken. So we got off Interstate 95 to follow the signs to the chicken place. It was supposed to be just a few short miles down the road. It was longer than we expected with just tall thin trees on either side of the road for a couple of turns and a few long miles. We bought some chicken and ate it on a picnic bench outside the establishment. When we finished, Fredrico asked me which way he should turn to get back to the freeway. I told him I thought you were supposed to remember the way back. I spent my time thinking about real country fried chicken; other than that, I was daydreaming, imagining that there might be some confederate soldiers left in "dem dare woods."

Well, it took us eight hours to find the interstate again. By this time we were in Savannah, Ga. at the other end of the state. We were a little more than halfway to our destination. When we crossed the Florida state line we stopped in a Welcome Center to get some free orange juice and use the toilet. When we got back in the car, Fredrico asked me to drive for a while. A few miles later we saw some guy hitchhiking down the road. He was a GI wearing an army uniform. I pulled over to pick him up and, after talking to the guy for a short time, Fredrico asked him if he wanted to get high. The guy said, "Sure." Fredrico pulled out some white powder and they both snorted it. I don't know how he knew that it would be all right to offer drugs to the guy. Maybe there is a code word that people in a secret network know about because I didn't even know Fredrico had drugs on him. It just reminded me why I was trying to get away from them and get a new start. We dropped the GI off at West Palm Beach and I was happy he was gone. I cannot stand people on drugs. It's a sign of weakness and shows me how inapt they are. We all know how addicting they are, so why start. I treat narcotics as if they are the forbidden fruit.

We arrived in Fort Lauderdale and found James and Ann's place. I knew where to go because when we went to Florida we always stayed at the same place. It was the Cotton Tail Motel on Sunrise Boulevard. I made myself at home that night. Fredrico stayed for about an hour and continued south to his Air Base. I told James what I wanted to do and he was okay with it. Ann didn't care either way. She was about eight and a half months pregnant and just wanted to have the baby and go back to Driftwood. James and I were going to try and make a living down there.

Fort Lauderdale is laid out like a grid. Broward Boulevard separates the city north and south and Andrews Avenue separates east from west. On Monday morning, James took me to the employment office and I found a job at a construction site as a helper building new homes. The site I worked at was SW 28th Street. Since I was staying on Sunrise Boulevard, that meant I had to travel about thirty blocks to get to work. James used his shipyard skills and welded gates for a fence company located on NE 40th Street. This was tough on him, as he had to drive me to work and then turn around and go to his job about seventy blocks away. Meanwhile, Ann was sitting alone at the motel waiting for the baby to come. Ann made friends with the owners of the place; I am sure that is why the owners didn't mind that another person was staying in their room. I didn't mind either. We were all family. Ann's motel bedroom was separated from the outer living area and that is where James and I stayed. One evening Ann wanted to go to the movie theater to see American Graffiti so I went with her. This was right before she had her baby. As we were walking down the boulevard, some guy riding by in a car whistled at her. Now, I don't know what is wrong with people. If I saw a woman and a guy and she was obviously pregnant, the last thing I would do is whistle at her. Ann took it in stride and kept walking as if nothing happened. It grossed me out.

I called Marie every other night. She said she was doing the same thing as before, only now when she finished cooking and cleaning she went out to the front porch, rocked in her rocking chair, and listened to her albums on her record player. She did this until the sun went down and then she went up and locked herself in her bedroom. About two weeks after I arrived in Florida, I asked her if she wanted to come down to stay with me. She said yes and asked her parents if she could go. Her parents didn't want her to come down alone and she was very uneasy about the move herself. She asked her second oldest brother Salvador (Sal) to come down with her. James and Sal worked at the Castleton Shipyard together and got along pretty well. I didn't care who brought her down, just as long as she came down. After another week, Marie and Sal boarded a plane and flew down to meet us. I was worried about how people were treating her while I was gone. Her house was very dull for a girl. They had a card table and a pool table in the dining room and no one ever played any music except Marie. Marie's only form of entertainment beside her albums was when she and her mother watched TV in the morning and evenings after the chores were done. Other than that, her mother sat in the kitchen and listened to her police band radio. Marie and I heard the radio and were annoyed by it when it periodically blurted out some code words or numbers.

I couldn't wait to see her. It had only been a few weeks, but it seemed a lot longer since we had been together.

When they finally arrived, James went to pick them up from the airport. It was the same Marie as before except her face was starting to break out. This didn't bother me but I was worried that something was upsetting her. That first night, after checking into our motel, Salvatore and James went out to a bar. Marie and I went to her room to be alone. I was happy and excited and she seemed to be in amazement just to be there. For Marie, it was a shock to go from Philadelphia to Fort Lauderdale in about two hours. We talked for a few minutes before we started to kiss and make out. It was great, just like before. When I got her on the floor and started to make love, it was just like the first time we ever did it. Phillip and Marie connected on all points that night. Afterward, Marie and I talked all night long. We didn't care about anything except each other. We really didn't need anything except each other to feel good. We would never use each other to vent anger about things that didn't go right in our lives. We knew that the most important thing in the world was that we had each other. From now on we would never be apart.

The next week her brother Sal flew back up to Pennsylvania and Marie moved in with Ann, James and me. From the first day, Marie and Ann got along very well. My sister knew the lifestyle her family lived. Ann's ex-husband Louie and Marie's father's family knew each other from the old neighborhood in Castleton.

The next week Ann had her baby. It was a girl and she named her Christina. She was a pretty girl. Ann was very strong and I wasn't surprised when I saw her just one hour after giving birth walking down the hall as if she was going to the movies. Marie, Ann, and I went to the nursery to see the newborn. A week later Chrisy's father, Petie came down and the three of them boarded a jet home. Petie went back to live with his mommy and daddy and Ann went back to our parent's house with Holly and Christina. Both little girls became an extension to the Webster family.

Marie's old man insisted we go to see this guy. His name was Bert Swann and he was in insurance sales and collection. He was a big strong man. He grew up in Castleton and moved down to Florida when he was a young man. He was a nice fellow. He and his wife came to our motel for a visit and invited us to his house for dinner. His wife was one of those people that, on your first meeting, hugs and kisses you on the lips. It kind of grossed me out since I didn't know the man, let alone his wife. It usually takes me about an hour just to look a female I first meet in the eyes. He was more realistic and just hugged Marie and told her how much she looked like her old man. Since James taught me how to drive his stick-shift Volkswagen Beetle, I was able to drive to Bert's house. Bert Bar-B-Q'ed us steak with corn on the cob and it was the first time I ever had a meal like this. It was really nice. We met his seven-year-old daughter. She was a little odd. She started to sing the theme song to the movie Bonnie and Clyde when we were near her. It took me a little while to guess, but I think she sang this tune because Bert told them about what the old man's family did and she thought we were some kind of criminals.

By September of 1973, James had a girlfriend living with her parents in Upper Manchester. She was the same girl he dated while he was in the Air Force and she went to Manchester High School and graduated a year after I did. She just turned eighteen but acted much older. James asked her to come down and we all shared a two-bedroom duplex in the Oakland Park section of the city. It was nice in this section of the city and convenient for James since it was about five blocks from his job.

There was a large park down the end of the block where local teams played softball games under the lights. It was late September by now, but still very warm. I liked the sunshine and warm breezes. I still worked at the construction site and by now most of the homes in the development were built. I worked steady and, although I arrived to work late sometimes, the boss liked me. He kept me on to mow the lawns of the new homes until they were purchased. Marie got a job at a Pizza Hut restaurant about a block away on Andrews Avenue. She enjoyed working there and getting tips again. Marie didn't look like the classic blonde or have a big body as my sister did, but men were attracted to her and they always gave her good tips. Unlike working in the old man's pizza shop, she also got a small paycheck to go with the tips. Things were going pretty good. My work was now about seventy city blocks away. James's girlfriend was staying with us and when James was still working, she would come to pick me up from work. One night after we got back to our place, James told me that I would have to find another way home. When I asked him why he said it was because Marie said something to his girlfriend about giving me a ride home. I asked Marie about it but she didn't tell me anything. She just said, "I don't like that bitch."

The next day I started to hitchhike to work. It wasn't easy, I walked to Andrews Avenue and hitched a ride usually to downtown and then walked through the business district and try to catch another ride the remaining twenty blocks to my job site. There were a few times when I just walked the rest of the way. It seemed at that time in the morning most people traveled in the other direction, towards downtown. One time when I first started to walk towards Andrews Avenue this man pulled over to pick me up. I told him where I wanted to go and he said, "If you want, get in, and I'll take you as far as downtown." He seemed like an okay guy so I got in with him. He was nice and we started to talk. He told me he was a stockbroker; as if that meant something to me. I told him I was a construction worker. He dressed well and drove a new Ford LTD. He said he was going downtown every day and I could ride with him if I wanted to. He said he lived nearby and saw me walking and hitchhiking in this same area before. He was going to pick me up but someone else did before him. He went on to say that I looked very tall standing there with my thumb out. I said that I was only six feet one inch tall and that I probably looked taller because I was thin. He reached across and put his hand on my stomach and lifted my shirt and while touching my bare belly he said, "You're not skinny at all." I didn't like this one bit and I said. "Let me out, right here!" He said, "I thought you were going to southwest Twenty Eight Street?" I said, "Yes, but I want to get out now." I started to open the door of his moving car and he pulled over and let me out. He said, "I didn't mean to upset you." I didn't say anything and got out and worried about being late for work. That night I went to Sears and bought a new Free Spirit ten-speed bike. A week later I was riding my bike home from work when the guy in the LTD pulled up next to me at a traffic light. He asked if I wanted to stop by his place on the way home and have a drink with him. I told him, "No, thank you."

James came home from work one day and told me that one of the fence installers needed a helper; so the next day I met the guy and he gave me a job. The next day I quit my job at the construction site and began installing fences with my new boss, Sherman the German. ❧

## Chapter 15: Two Became One and Then Became Three

It was late October when Marie said she needed to go to a doctor because she was having some female problems. She came home from the doctor and told me she was pregnant. Here we go again; what in the hell was I going to do now? Marie's prescription for birth control pills ran out so she stopped taking them. I couldn't remember the specific time we had sex that could have resulted in her getting pregnant, but I knew my rhythm method had holes in it. Well, there was no question on what to do next. I needed to start saving money for the doctor. Marie told me that she wanted to go to the same doctor as Ann. We called his office and he accepted Marie as a patient. He wanted the payment upfront since I didn't have any insurance. The doctor fee was only a few hundred dollars and, besides this, I had to pay the hospital about six hundred dollars and they both wanted their money in six weeks. It wasn't a problem at the time because Marie and I were both working and my brother James and I shared the rent, food and utility bills.

Christmas was coming soon and we wanted to go back up north to celebrate the holy day with our families. Marie was starting to show so we decided to get married. In the state of Florida, we had to go downtown to the Broward County Courthouse and pay for a license and get a blood test. In my mind, getting married was only a piece of paper to keep others happy. My lifetime commitment to Marie started a long time ago; when she gave up drugs to be with only me. Marie wanted to get married by the state, so we did. We found a small Wedding Chapel on the old Dixie Highway to make our promise to each other. Marie invited a friend from work. He ˄ll right guy; about eighteen-years-old and originally ıt. Like us, he came down to Florida with his to start a life of their own. We got along when we first met and he and I would go down to the park and play tag football with the locals on Sundays. Marie and his girlfriend would walk around Oakland Park talking and enjoying the nice weather. He and his girlfriend attended the wedding along with Bert and his wife. James and his girlfriend were our witnesses as we entered into the Holy Estate of Matrimony. Marie bought a new green dress at Sears and I purchased a new shirt and borrowed a sports jacket from James for the ceremony. The official at the chapel was a German émigré with a thick accent. Marie and I could hardly understand him. I was more nervous about having to repeat what he said than getting married. It didn't take long for us to consent together to Holy Wedlock. The whole day was very nice and I felt good about it.

My wife and I flew up to Philadelphia that night. When we got to her house, the old man met me in the living room and shook my hand and congratulated me on marrying his daughter. This made me feel pretty good. After we visited my family, we went back to her house and walked right upstairs and into her old bedroom and slept together. Everything was just how she left it. No one was allowed to touch anything of hers after she moved to Florida. The next day the old man took us to see his mother in Castleton. She gave us a wedding gift of fifty one-dollar bills. We celebrated Christmas and New Year's with our families and then we returned to Fort Lauderdale.

Working for the fence company was fun. I liked going to different places every day to install fences. I worked with this man named Sherman Rush. He was a physically large man with a balding dome and long light-colored hair on the sides. His full reddish beard gave him a Viking appearance. He was an intelligent man in his work preparation and had every job figured out before we reach the job site. After getting to know him, he told me how he had to quit his well paying job as a grocery store chain sales representative in New Jersey. He went on to say that he came to Florida to win his wife back. See, his wife got pregnant by another man and left Sherman for the man and ran away with him to Fort Lauderdale. The man eventually left her and the baby. She was alone but still would not take Sherman back.

That didn't stop Sherman from going to her apartment every other day and leaving milk and pampers for her baby. It made me think of how a man so big and strong with high intelligence could still be controlled by someone that was so mean to him.

James' girlfriend started to work at the same Pizza Hut as Marie and this bothered Marie. My wife didn't like this girl at all. Marie would fight with her sometimes and throw cups and things like that at her. I didn't pay much attention to this and hoped it would go away in time. James knew how Marie and her family dealt with some issues and tolerated what was happening just as I did. The girl went to Manchester and should have known who she was dealing with, but she didn't. James' girlfriend was scared all the time. She came to me one day and asked, "Why doesn't Marie like me?"

I didn't have an answer. I said, "Try not to piss her off."

She said, "This last time Marie got pissed, I only asked her, why do you always receive more tips than me?"

I said, "What did Marie say?" She just threw a spoon at me and said, "That's why, you dumb fucking bitch, you."

Marie and I would go for a walk around our new neighborhood almost every night. We would talk about a lot of things, nothing important mostly just walking and talking it was relaxing for me when we were alone together. I would tell her about the Sunshine State. And how it was building up and a lot of people from up north lived there now. She would make comments like, "Yea, it's nice, but the rednecks forgot to build sidewalks." I did not have a response because she was right; there were hardly any sidewalks around the neighborhoods.

Just her and I was how we liked it most, just the two of US, a couple of nobodies from nowhere. She was the Unsure, Uncertain, and Urban, in our relationship and I was the Sure, Safe, and Smart one. We would talk about small things; never anything too personal or about the past. There were times she would drop hints about how bad it was growing up with her old man but would stop short of saying anything too revealing. She told me that once when she was six-years-old some man-made her get in a car with him and he took her to the Delaware River and threatened to throw her in the river if she didn't do what he said. I never asked for details. I too like to live in the moment.

We enjoyed the warm peaceful night air. Everything was new and clean here. No noise from the steam valves of Sun Oil. We didn't have to see the clouds of steam and smoke coming from the units of the refinery. No more smell of burnt crude oil. The refinery was no longer a daily reminder of what could have been.

I liked my job and I was good at it. It was easy, like digging in soft dirt with a little sand mixed in. To install the fence post all you had to do was run a string from point to point and mark off every ten feet, take three or four stabs in the ground with the post hole diggers and you had a three-foot hole to stick a fence post in it. When it was time, I would mix the cement, pour it in the hole around the post, and then level it and that was about it. Sherman and I would come back the next day after the cement hardened and hang the chain link and the job was done. The wooden fences were even easier. You didn't have to mix cement, just run the string, set the post, tamp the dirt back into the hole, nail the panels to the post, and presto - you had a fence! Wooden fences could be done in one day.

When Marie was five months pregnant she quit her job. Everything was going well. I would take Marie to her doctor's appointments and the pregnancy went fine. By April, she was seven months pregnant and was getting big. My brother, John, and my sisters, Mary and Joan, came down to visit us during the Easter holiday. We all went to the movies to see The Exorcist. After watching all the hoopla caused by the previews, I wasn't in a big hurry to see this movie. At John's insistence, we went anyhow, and the night we went to the movie theater it was so packed that we couldn't sit together. I volunteered to stay out but they insisted I go in to see it with them. Well, it scared the crap out of me. I would walk through Castleton with Marie at two in the morning on a hot summer night before I would open my eyes to watch this. The scariest part for me was when the possessed little girl started to talk like a man. That hit me to the core. When she turned her head completely around, I just closed my eyes. I didn't want to be there any longer. I walked up the aisle to where Marie was sitting. I tried to get her to leave the theater with me because I didn't want our unborn baby to sense the terror caused by such evil. Marie liked it, she wasn't leaving for anyone. I am sure she would just smack the little brat across the face just to see how many times the devil girl's head would spin around. She would then tell her, "Your mother sucks little red dog's cocks in hell." That night lying in bed was the only time I remember wanting to sleep with the lights on. I was severely rattled.

It was summer and the time for Marie to have the baby was getting close. My mom and dad came down and so did her mom. It was the first time her mother was out of the state of Pennsylvania and the first time on an airplane. Her mom stayed in our room with Marie and my parents stayed at a motel. I slept out in the living room. This was only the third grandchild for my parents and the eighth one for her mom. Everyone was excited for us. Her mom shared her worries and concerns about Marie having a baby so far away from where they lived as if Castleton was the center of the universe. My mom tried to assure Mrs. Volpe that Fort Lauderdale had good doctors and hospitals too. That didn't stop her from worrying about Marie every day and every night and asking me why I wanted to live so far away.

In early June, we all went to a restaurant that offered a smorgasbord for dinner. I could hardly eat but Marie ate everything on the menu. She had seconds and thirds. After dinner, James took my mom and dad back to where they were staying and that is when Marie's water broke and she started having contractions. We didn't have a phone but the landlady who lived next door did. She allowed us to call the motel where my mother and father were staying. We asked the clerk to give my parents the message that Marie was ready to go and we needed Jimmy to give her a ride to the hospital. It wasn't far and he came back right away. Marie was in good hands with my mother and hers. Between the two of them, they had twenty-four babies.

Also, my mom was a nurse. Because Marie used to walk around without shoes or socks, her feet were dirty. Her mother spent the time waiting for James by washing Marie's feet saying, "How could you even think of going to the hospital with dirty feet?"

Broward General Hospital was about thirty-five blocks away but straight down Andrews Avenue. It was around eight p.m. so traffic wasn't bad. James drove Marie, her mom, and I to the hospital in plenty of time. James returned to give our parents a ride to the hospital. The nurses took Marie right into the maternity ward. Her mom and I stayed in the waiting room. This hospital had a policy not to allow anyone except the doctors, nurses, and patient into the delivery room. Me, my Mom, Dad, and Mrs.Volpe had to wait until the baby was delivered before we were allowed to see the new mother and child. It took about two hours waiting in one area before Mrs. Volpe, my parents, and I were moved to another smaller room, closer to the delivery room. Once, when a hospital emergency team came by with some medical equipment on wheels, Mrs. Volpe began to freak out, saying, "Marie's going to die in there." My mom had to settle her down by saying, "We don't even know if the emergency equipment is for Marie or not." Then Mrs. Volpe said that when she had her last baby she almost died on the delivery table.

We kept asking the desk nurse how it was going and the reply was always, "Things are going fine. We will let you know when the baby arrives."

Another hour later, this short, heavy-set, Black nurse came out with this big smile on her face. She asked if the father was here to see his newborn baby. This lady let me in and she had this genuine smile on her face from ear to ear. I figured that she helped deliver a hundred babies before, but this one pleased her a lot. She picked up my son and said look how big he is. And he was, he weighed nine pounds and seven ounces and was just as healthy as could be.

I was led into the next room and saw Marie lying on the bed exhausted saying, "I had to tell them the baby was coming out. They left me in a room by myself. I was able to reach down to feel his head coming out with my hand and they told me not to touch it. Then they gave me some medicine and it knocked me out."

I said, "Did you see the baby yet."

"No! Not yet."

I said, "It's a boy."

She said, "That's wonderful," and I said, "You did a wonderful job, Marie."

Marie and I named our son, Phillip Jr. After a week, Marie's mom caught a return flight to Driftwood and my parents left a few days later. For two months, when I came home from work, I would lie down on the living room floor with my son lying on my chest. Our hearts beating next to each other as he'd sleep on my chest as I watched TV. After dinner, we would take walks with Phillie down to the park and sometimes we would use the public payphone to call up north. Marie talked to her family and everyone asked when she was coming home. They all wanted to see the baby. I wasn't making a lot of money at my job, so we couldn't just hop on a plane and fly up there very often. James worked in the weld shop and got a steady paycheck. My work was not as steady but James knew how much or how little work I had that week, so if I was paid less and didn't have enough money for our share of the rent, he knew why. I never missed a day of work and considered it an insult to myself and my family if I didn't give a full effort every day. I was twenty years old now and had a wife and a baby to support and wasn't going to let them down.

Marie would talk on the payphone to her family for an hour and, as time passed, I would stand by and watch the lacrosse players practice in the park. Occasionally, I would drift near the phone to try and listen to her. I could tell her family kept hounding her to come home to live with them. I hated that. Marie didn't like it either. During our walks, we would talk about how nice it was in Fort Lauderdale. Nobody knew us and no one cared where we were from or who we were related to. We liked being a couple of nobodies from nowhere. We could start a new life. We only needed to be left alone. I told Marie that I thought James and I could start our own fence crew. We would make a good team, he was smart and wasn't afraid of a little hard work.

Marie finally gave in to her family and announced that she wanted to return to Driftwood. I was very, very disappointed and told her so. I said that I wanted to stay in Florida.

She said, "We don't even have a phone of our own. What are we going to do if the baby gets sick?"

"Take him to the doctor," I said.

"What are we going to do if you lose your job?"

I said, "Find a new one."

"How are we going to get a car for ourselves?"

"I'll save up the money and buy one."

"When are we going to get a place of our own?"

"We will get a place of our own when we can afford it," I answered.

I could tell her family was using our present conditions to pressure her. She couldn't fight them anymore.

I pleaded, "Just try to stay with me, we will work it out. Look around you, and smell the freedom." She didn't respond to my pleas. The next day, her old man sent her a plane ticket and she and our baby flew back to them. James and his girlfriend took my wife and my child to the airport. Marie asked if I was going to go to the airport to see them off. I said, "No."

I stayed in my room thinking, "Oh, Marie how could you do this to us? We are one against all your past oppression. How can you go back to them? What kind of a hold do they have on you? What did they say to you that can come between us? Where is your love for me? Is it less than your love for them? We are companions, isn't that what we grew together on? Is the magnetism to them more than the bond that we shared these last years? What we created is our son, isn't he ours together? You have to know I would not allow my seed to come close to anyone that I didn't love. You are the only person I gave all my love and the rights to my family name. My very soul is yours, where are you taking us? Is my son, who we created, is he better with them? How can this be? What have I done to deserve this? Don't you know that our dream can come true? I will follow you. I have to suffer this loss alone before I can return to a life of failure. They will not raise my son. EVER!"

I worked and stayed home without calling her until the next week. My heart was cold without the warmth of our infant lying on my chest. I called to ask how everything was and if our baby was okay?

She asked, "Are you coming up to be with us?"

I said. "I still think we should try to make a life for ourselves down here, but I will come up next week to visit."

I didn't tell her exactly when I would come up to see her and Phillie. Three weeks after they left me, I flew up to Pennsylvania. I worked that day and got into Philadelphia late. In those days, it took about two hours and about seventy-five dollars for a flight from Fort Lauderdale Hollywood Airport to Philadelphia. I caught a cab to Driftwood and by the time the cab driver pulled over to let me out, it was about midnight. Her brothers were hanging out in front of the house with a couple of their friends. I felt as though I was returning to the dark ages. I couldn't even look at them when I asked if Marie was awake. One of them said, "Yea, go on up to see her." As if I needed their permission to go and see my wife and son. That same guy that was obsessed with Marie said, "She is waiting for you." I didn't like the way he said that. It seemed like he knew everything she was doing.

The reunion went all right, nothing special, just that Marie was glad to see me and I felt a little more relaxed about the situation when I was with her. I just wanted to be with her and our baby. Phillie was doing well. Marie already took him to one of their doctors for a checkup. These people were so narrow-minded that even doctors from another state are suspect.

When I was with Marie, she talked about getting an apartment for us in Penn's Port. The thought of living there depressed me. I flew back to Florida the next night. The short flight magnified the difference between Driftwood and Fort Lauderdale.

When I was visiting Marie and my son, she said that a week earlier my mom had called her over to her house and asked if she would bring the baby with her. My family wanted to see him and give him some gifts. My mom asked Marie, "When are you returning to Florida?" Marie replied that she didn't know.

I knew Marie was serious about staying up north no matter what I did. I waited another two weeks and made plans to move back to Pennsylvania. First, I asked my brother John if he would come and help James out with the rent. John was free and still living at home. He didn't have a career or a steady girlfriend so it was easy for him to move around. I flew back to Pennsylvania and the first thing I did was to go over to talk to my parents about my situation. My mom wanted me to leave her. She said, "Once she leaves you for her family, she will always choose her family over you. Get out now before you spend your entire life being second best." My dad said, "What she did to you was wrong, but your son is with her and you should be with your wife and your son." I agreed with my Dad. ∾

## Chapter 16: Back to the Scene of the Crime

I dreaded moving back home. I felt like such a loser, especially moving to an apartment in the borough of Penn's Port. People in Driftwood looked down on very few people in this world and one was Castleton folks and the other was our neighbors in Penn's Port. The refineries made the whole town smell bad. The Delaware River was polluted and only good for shipping and waste disposal. The place had more than its share of derelicts living in one-room apartments.

It only had a population of around 2,000 residents, in spite of all that, it produced two popular professional athletes. I already mentioned Mickey Vernon and the other is Blazing Billy Johnson, a professional football player.

By the end of September 1974, there I was, living at One West 10th Street, Penn's Port, Pennsylvania. Marie's brother, Matthew, and his wife, Virginia, and their one-year-old son, little Matty, already lived in Penn's Port about a block away. I liked Virginia. She was from the other side of Driftwood and went to Holy Sacrament and Manchester about a year ahead of me. By this time, Marie's mom worked at the Salvation Army Store in Penn's Port. That is how we furnished our apartment. We had a used couch, used dresser drawers, and even a used kitchen set. Everything you needed was right there in the Salvation store for the taking. Her family took the first grabs on everything. A person would call up to donate something and they would go to the person's house and if they liked it they would bring it straight to whoever wanted it. They would pick out the best for themselves. This was the first time I ever had a color television. At first, it didn't work, but then Popeye bought some new tubes and it worked almost as good as new. Still, the only color was green and it flickered and flipped a lot but it wasn't just a plain old black and white television. The Websters never had a color television in the house while I lived there.

Our two-story building had two apartments on the second floor, us and our neighbors, a single mother and her eleven-year-old son. We sat above a doctor's office, dry cleaners, and a barbershop. The main entrance to our apartment was from an alley. The steps leading from the alley were enclosed. At the top of the steps were two doors, ours and our neighbor's. The living room was small. In the middle of our apartment was the kitchen and all the other rooms were off of that. We put our bedroom on the street side and Phillie's cradle was in our room. We had two spare rooms, one next to the front bedroom and the other on the far side of the kitchen. Out the back door from the kitchen was a fire escape. This would take you down to a walkway and either out to the sidewalk on Tenth Street or to the back parking lot of the Quaker Meat Market. I wouldn't exactly call it a neighborhood, but the area wasn't bad, and we knew most of the locals. Sure the local chapter of the Heathens motorcycle club used Penn's Port as its headquarters, but we knew a few members so we were able to get along with them most of the time. You would be fine around them just as long as you didn't tell them to go take a bath, or if you rode some sissy motorbike. I once saw them sic their two Doberman Pincers dogs on some poor bastard who unfortunately stopped his 50cc Honda motorcycle at a red light.

Penn's Port's main drag was Interstate Route 33. The road has been around since the 1700s and, at that time, it was known as Post Road. A lot of heavy traffic passed below our bedroom window. Mostly, they were trucks going north to Castleton, Pa. or south to Wilmington, Del.

Our apartment became the Volpes' headquarter in Penn's Port, at least for the younger ones. Almost every day someone from up at the Volpe's house would call down and ask if we needed something from the store and, if so, Popeye used to come down and drop it off and hang out for a while. Marie's younger sisters Silvia, Olivia, and Monica would come down to help Marie with the baby nearly every day. In the evenings, the older brothers would come in and chase the younglings' away saying, "Go home, mommy wants you to get home right away." All they had to do was walk up Green Street and across the bridge over the railroad tracks and they were a block away from home.

I really did try to find work but couldn't. After a month, Matthew helped me get a job where he worked at a cement factory in Castleton. I rode to work with him. They only paid minimum wage, but it was a job. The first week they had me repair patches on cracked cement blocks used in the building of skyscrapers. The next week I was put in the sandblast department. The sandblasting hose has 90 pounds per square inch of air pressure blowing sand out the end and it was a bitch trying to maneuver that thing. The dust would blind you after about two seconds of blasting. While operating the sandblaster, you needed heavy clothing to protect yourself from the ratcheted sand. The sand grains still managed to get through and sting the shit out of you. I was supposed to lightly wash off the smooth surface of the finished concrete to show the stones in the cement for texture and appearance. A couple of times I left the hose in one area longer than I should have and it started to bore a hole in the cement block. I got laid off after four weeks of work.

Sometimes, when the refineries would have what they called a "shut down," a lot of us locals would go to the side gate and stand in front of the subcontractor's trailer. The foreman would come out about 6:30 a.m. and pick out men to come in the gate to do the dirty work the regular refinery employees wouldn't do. All kinds of men were out there, some from Castleton but mostly from Manchester. I didn't get picked the first time I went, but I got aggressive the next time standing in front of other men to get noticed by the boss. The next day I went back I was picked again, but unfortunately, the work didn't last more than a couple of weeks. The refineries shut down every six months. So when we heard about it we would go back to work for a few weeks. The pay was good but nowhere near what the regular Oil Workers got. Sometimes we would have to work the graveyard shift from 11 p.m. till 7 a.m. Whenever I did this, a couple of Marie's sisters or maybe her little brother Joey would stay the night at our place. I didn't mind. It made me feel as though she was safer when someone was with her. Gerald, got hired at the same time I did as subcontractors at BP Refinery.

On January 31, 1975, Gerald and I were working the graveyard shift. We were standing at the job site with a couple of other guys waiting to be lifted up to the top of the reactor. We would have to go up to the top and climb inside to clean the small particle of catalyst that became lodged in the filter screens. All of a sudden, we heard this crunching of metal sound immediately followed by a massive explosion. This was followed by two successive loud blasts. I instantly turned and ran in the other direction. I turned to see the other three, including Gerald, scattered in different directions. I didn't know what the fuck was going on. I looked towards the ball of fire and realized that Marie and Phillie were closer than I was to the massive blaze. I continued to run out of the back gate of the refinery and headed straight for our apartment. I thought about Gerald as I passed BP's main gate. I saw a group of employees and realized that must be where the employees muster during an emergency. I went back in through the main gate and saw that Gerald was fine. He said he was going down towards the river to see exactly what happened. He said they thought it was an oil tanker explosion. I told him I was going to see if Marie was all right and to tell the boss if he asked where I went.

I was about four blocks from our apartment and Marie and Phillie. I ran all the way. People were coming out of their houses wondering what had just happened. Growing up around there, everyone knew at any time an explosion could happen. As I got closer to Marie and Phillie, I could tell that they were out of range of the fire, but I knew she would worry about me if I didn't come to see her. As I passed the business section of Penn's Port on Tenth Street, I could see the hardware store windows had broken from the concussion of the blast. The burglar alarms in both banks on the corner of Tenth and Market were ringing and the volunteer fire company's sirens were blaring. I made it to our apartment and no one was there so I called her parents' house to see if she was with them and she was. I told her I was okay and that I would come up to be with them.

As I walked up Market Street, the local Friendship Fire Company trucks passed me heading towards the enormous blaze. It had become a ten-alarm fire by now including all the surrounding fire companies. When I saw Marie, she told me that she was lying down with little Phillie. She was trying to fall asleep when this loud explosion ripped through the apartment blowing the curtains in from the windows. Even though it was January, we left the windows partially open because the heat coming up from the dry cleaners below would always heat our apartment. Marie was afraid and didn't have a clue as to what was happening. She told me that she wanted to wait to see if I was okay, but her family insisted that she go up to their house to do that.

I wasn't surprised Marie was up at her mom's because, besides seeing the flames and hearing the explosion, the Volpes knew most of the details about every emergency that was going on around the county. That is because at any hour of the day or night someone in the house was awake listening to the police scanner. Some people said that is how Mrs. Volpe kept track of her boys. When the old lady went to bed Popeye would take over listening to it. They knew every code word and number the dispatcher would use. Penn's Port that night seemed like it was noon instead of midnight. People were outside along Hampton Road looking down on Penn's Port as they always did. I walked over to the Webster's house to let Mom and Dad know that Gerald and I were all right. Fire trucks from all over Delaware County were on the scene. The fire took a few days to extinguish. The news said, "The Oil tanker Corinthos, docked at the BP oil refinery, was rammed by the merchant ship Edgar M. Queeny while heading south on the Delaware River."

Some of the crew-members were blown a hundred yards away, body parts landed on the barrel-house in the refinery. A nearby gay club burnt to the ground. Bodies of merchant marines were found days later floating down the river as far as Wilmington,

Delaware. Twenty-nine officers and crew, all foreigners, perished horribly that night.

After a few weeks, I was laid off by the subcontractor in the refinery and things around town returned to normal. I was always trying to find a job. As soon as any one of my or Marie's brothers heard of a place was hiring, we would all go and fill out an application. There was a lot of industry in the area and we would go anywhere from DuPont Chemical Co. in Edgemore, Delaware to the Castleton Ship Yard looking for work. Shamefully, I was collecting welfare at the time and was desperate to find work. It was the mid-seventies and times were tough all over.

A few of Marie's brothers would come down to our apartment and I would stay up late and play board and card games all night. We played Risk and Monopoly. Marie and I had a record player and played music like the Steve Miller Band or Electric Light Orchestra. Sometimes they would bring a friend. This person usually had some money to buy beer and or bring pot to smoke. I started to smoke pot at this time. I rekindled my loser attitude from grade school and began to not give a shit about anything. We would sit in my kitchen and play games and bullshit till dawn. Occasionally, Samuel would enlighten us by explaining things like how the game of basketball was invented. He said that the ancient Mexicans cut their prisoners of war heads off and threw it through a hole in a wall.

One night, Popeye brought this guy in to join us. We hardly knew him but learned he received a disability check from the government for his injuries he received in Vietnam. He was a local guy that went to Manchester High School a year or so ahead of me. Because he had money to buy beer and pot, Popeye brought him in. I never used any kind of hard drugs, but that wasn't the case for them, especially Popeye.

About three o'clock in the morning, while we were sitting at my kitchen table playing cards, Popeye's buddy started to go into convulsions. He started easy enough, just nodding his head but ended up on the floor flopping around like he wanted to show everybody how stiff and straight he could get his body. Fredrico began to give Popeye a hard time for bringing this fool into the apartment. The guy started to worry me because I thought perhaps he was going to die. If that happened, I would have to deal with the police and I didn't want that. Samuel jumped up and said, "If this guy is going to act like that, he's got to go." Samuel and Fredrico lifted him up and dragged him out the back door and put him onto the fire escape. There he lay completely motionless and unconscious about five feet from my back door. I really got worried, so I said, "We have to do something." Samuel said as he sat there sucking saliva through his front teeth, "Call the cops and report a prowler, they'll come and cart him away." Fredrico said, "No, don't call the cops, just leave him there; the night air would do him good." Believe it or not about ten minutes later, when I looked out my back door he was gone. I never saw the guy again.

A couple of months later, Fredrico got a job at Iron Box, a steel fabrication shop in Castleton. They just got a contract to build some outfitting items for the shipyard and needed helpers. Marie called from her mom's and told me about the opportunity so I walked up to their house in Driftwood. I asked Popeye if he wanted to drive down there and fill out an application. Popeye asked the old man exactly where this place was located. He said it was down on Second and Highland Avenue near the electric power plant. We drove down there and looked all over for the place and couldn't find it. Later, I asked Fredrico where it was and he said, "Forget about it, you wouldn't want to work there anyhow, the bosses were mean bastards." I was on welfare at the time and did not care how mean the bosses were, I needed a job. I didn't have to say that to him because he already knew it.

About three weeks later, Samuel asked me to drive him down so we could pick Fredrico up from work. When we got there, I found out that it wasn't at 2nd and Highland but instead directly across the street from their grandparent's house. This same steel fabrication shop had been at this location since the old man lived there. This upset me; I needed a job real bad, but because it was next to where the family did business, the old man didn't want me near it.

The old man was a very controlling person. He would insist that we go up to his house whenever we needed anything like to wash our clothes and especially for Sunday dinner, which was always the same, spaghetti and meatballs. Mrs. Volpe made her sauce the night before. The meatballs were made that morning and their family always ate dinner around one o'clock in the afternoon. I didn't like her spaghetti, so Marie would make me an Italian sausage sandwich. They must have hated me just for that. No one talked bad about her spaghetti, but I wouldn't eat it and I never did.

In the fall, while Marie helped around the kitchen, I would go out with the boys to try and find a tackle football game. We would go anywhere we heard that guys played tackle football. We would go to the east end of Castleton or the west end, it didn't matter. We'd go to Delaware if we heard they had a good game. Samuel was the best player and Carlo their younger brother was maturing into a force himself. These guys would tackle anyone without hesitation. I don't know how they did it. They would swoop in and knock the runner on his ass. It didn't matter how big the person or his reputation. They would hit him on his thigh and not even wrap their hands around the guy's legs and the ball carrier went down.

They surprised a lot of people by performing above their size. Once they beat the living shit out of a big Black guy from Castleton. Samuel, Carlo, and their friend Wally Storm were listening to the Flyers hockey game on their radio in a local bar. The unfortunate guy came into the bar and said the radio was too loud. Samuel started it by smashing the radio in the guy's face. That was it, the fight was on. They beat that man all the way into the ambulance. And then some more after he was laying on the gurney.

Not long after that, a guy who went to school with my brother James, named Willy Judd, asked me about what happened.

Will was a bear, about six foot four and two hundred and forty pounds. A few years earlier he played college football with the guy the Volpes beat up. He said he wouldn't want to have to fight this guy for any reason. He also asked me how the hell did guys, as small as the Volpes were, hurt someone as big and tough as his ex-teammate? I told him I had no idea except that they do stuff like that all the time. I did not witness the beating firsthand, but I believed Samuel when he told me about it. Later, when he was arrested for assault and battery with mayhem, he needed money to get bailed out of jail. Someone called Marie and asked if we had any money so they could get Sammy out of County Jail. They always said stuff like, he is married and has a wife and four kids, including the twins born a year earlier, to take care of. Everyone knew that his wife, Pat, and their kids lived with her parents and Samuel still lived at home. About a week later we sent up sixty dollars. The Volpes didn't have any assets because they already had their house on bond for someone else. A short time later, I went with Samuel to see his lawyer. I was sitting next to Samuel while he and the lawyer talked about the case. Samuel said he didn't have any money to pay his fee right now. The lawyer said, "Don't worry about it, but just so you know my daughter plays tennis." It took me a while, but the best I can infer from the lawyer's statement is that the bastard wanted us to burglarize a sporting goods store and give him some tennis gear.

Marie's brothers were nervous and on edge all the time but showed no fear when it came to fighting someone. Once while Samuel and his friend Wally Storm were eating at a new hoagie shop in Penn's Port operated by the Heathen's Motor Cycle Club Samuel started complaining to the girl who made the sandwich about how bad it tasted. I never went in their store so I wouldn't know, but I am sure it was the fact that a non-Italian was working in a hoagie shop that prompted this outburst. Samuel was a proud Italian and it seemed to me that for every beer he drank his Italian accent got more profound. Well, before too long the girls' called down to the clubhouse and in entered a couple of bikers and the fight was on. Skinny-ass Wally Storm ran down to Matthew's house to get help. By the time it was all over, Samuel and one biker ended up in the hospital.

Meanwhile, still in Florida, my brother Jimmy and his girlfriend had a baby girl and named her Summer. Not a real Catholic name, but we all loved her just the same. Soon after that, James, his girlfriend, and the baby, along with my brother John returned to Pennsylvania. I should have stayed in closer touch with them, but I didn't. Good old Nana passed away in the winter of 1974. The night before she died, I went to see her in the hospital. She was a good woman and I am sorry I wasn't nicer to her. She did her best with us sons of bitches and bastards.

Not long after that, my brother John joined the Army. That's right, good old John at age 23, was signing up to protect the nation. By now, it was late 1974 and the chance of going to combat was slim to none. The Army was offering deals to recruits like if they join now they can pick their duty station. John wanted to go to Germany so he signed up. We were all proud of him. Gerald, Joan, Alice Carr, (John's "girlfriend" from kindergarten), Marie and I went down to South Carolina to see his graduation from Boot Camp. As it turned out, he couldn't go to Germany but they offered him a chance to go to Hawaii and he took it.

Marie's second oldest brother, Sal, sold us his car for one hundred dollars. He let us pay him in twenty-dollar payments. The car was a 1967 Pontiac Le Mans. A pretty cool car when it was new. Soon after I got it, the carburetor started to act up. I didn't know anything about cars so I asked Fredrico to help tune it up. It worked all right for a while, but soon the carburetor started to cause the car to stall out at red lights. Someone told me that it needed more air so I removed the air filter from around the carburetor and this seemed to work for a while. I would stop at a traffic light and put the car in neutral and give it gas so it didn't conk out. Once when we were leaving her house, the fucking thing caught on fire. I heard this puff like it backfired out the carburetor. I opened the hood and flames were coming out of the engine. I turned off the engine and the fire went out. Marie, carrying Phillie, got out and we all walked back to get a ride home from the old man. I asked Fredrico if he would help me work on it and we got it running again. After this happened to me a couple of times, the car had a big scorch mark on the middle of the front hood. I was beginning to think this car of mine was possessed by the devil or something. I sandpapered it smooth and covered it with grey paint primer from an aerosol spray can. The vinyl roof covering was peeling off so I scraped the rest off and sanded it smooth and put the same grey primer on it. Believe it or not, this did not make the car stand out too much, at least not in our neighborhood.

Fredrico was one of the few Volpes smarter than I was. He would usually win when we played cards or Risk but that did not stop him from coming up with some brainless comments. Once, he was wearing a pair of pants his mom got from the Salvation Army. They must have been irregulars from the manufactures or something like that because one leg was twisted. The seam of the left leg should have been to the outside just like the right leg and most other pants, but it wasn't, this seam was twisted around to the front. One evening he came downstairs wearing these pants and proclaimed, "Hey, look at these pants, they must have been tailor-made for a polio victim." Stuff like that happened all the time. Samuel wouldn't let his wife Pat take a bath while she was pregnant. He was afraid she would drown the unborn baby. These guys weren't very smart but they could get the girls. There was this urban legend about stray females coming into their house and not coming out for weeks. I did have a sighting once. One morning, I saw what looked like a strange female exiting out the front door. When I asked Marie about it, she told me it was possibly one of her brother's new "girlfriends." She went on to say, if one of her brothers got a girl he would take her upstairs to the third floor and screw her a few times and then pass her around to the rest of his brothers. They would call up Anthony and Matthew to come up and get a piece of ass while it was still around. Once a girl came in the house on a Friday and did not leave until the next Tuesday. Another time, when they were done with a girl, Sal asked Marie if she would give the girl some clothes. Evidently, the poor gal lost track of all her clothes including her underwear.

I drove the Pontiac until it literally fell apart. We were going to our apartment after washing our clothes at her parents' house and I was driving over the Penn's Port Bridge. When I reached the peak and started on the downhill side it collapsed on itself. The emergency breaks engaged and I came to an immediate stop. I pulled over to the side as much as I could so I didn't block traffic. They told me later that the A-frame broke and the car fell on top of the chassis. I had to pay a tow truck almost as much as it cost me to buy the car to move it off the road and to a junkyard.

Work started again at PP Kelley's, the subcontractor for BP oil refinery. This time the work lasted for a few months and I was able to get off welfare. I was on it for almost eight months. I hated being on it but I didn't seem to care enough to do anything about it at the time. Matthew knew this guy who needed bail money to get out of jail. He wanted to sell his car to get the money. I had some money from my income tax return. They told me it was a good deal so I bought it for two hundred bucks. It was a tan 1967 Plymouth Fury with a black vinyl top. It was less than perfect because it would shut off every time I made a sharp turn or a sudden stop. Fredrico told me that was because one of the motor mounts was broken and the engine would shift causing it to shut down. I didn't have a clue what a motor mount was so I decided to take wide turns everywhere I went and stop very slowly. This wasn't hard to do since most of the time I drove like an old lady.

My third oldest sister, Katherine, met and married a man named Wayne Sutter. Wayne was hanging around with James at the time that he was introduced to Katherine. He was a great guy and everyone liked him. He was employed at BP and was a hard worker. After he converted to Catholicism, they got married. We all went to their wedding at Holy Sacrament Church. It was really nice and they made a good couple.

The Volpe girls were always at our place. We treated them all right and they liked playing with Phillie. Especially Olivia and Monica enjoyed hanging out with us. The girls would stay most weekends and didn't like going home on Sunday afternoons. Silvia would not come down as much because she replaced Marie as the surrogate mother on Hampton Road. Around this time,

Marie's first younger brother, Carlo, was hanging around Penn's Port and would stop by to see Marie. He did this mostly when I was at work. He knew I didn't have a bank account at the time because I didn't want the government to know how much money I had. So, instead of a bank, I would go to a Cheese Steak shop down by the river to cash my paychecks. I kept most of my cash including my rent money in a book in the bedroom. One time Marie asked me to loan Carlo some money until he could pay me back, so I did. He saw me go to the bedroom to get the money and, without thinking; I let him see where I stashed the cash. I loaned him the money and he quickly paid me back.

About three weeks later, I was working second shift for PP Kelley's and Marie was up at her parent's house. When I got home from picking up Marie we noticed that our apartment was broken into. The door had two locks attached to the wooden frame around the door. The locks and door frame were no match for the burglar who must have forcefully kicked the door causing the vertical wooden frame to detach from the wall allowing the burglars entry. I quickly checked the place out and went straight to the book to see if our rent money was still there and it was gone. I was livid. Other than the doorframe lying broke on the living room floor and our rent money taken, nothing else was disturbed. No one lived next to us at the time, so whoever it was could walk up the enclosed stairs from the alley take their time and break in unnoticed and take what they wanted. I was so pissed off I grabbed a hammer and went outside to look for someone that might have broken into my apartment. I walked out from the alley onto Tenth Street and saw a car full of people looking at me. I waved my fist holding the hammer at them and asked, "What the hell you are looking at?" I stared at them as they drove away. After they passed, I walked around the corner to see if anyone saw what happen to my apartment. No one was around. I remembered that I didn't check well enough in each room so whoever did this deed may still be in the apartment with Marie and Phillie. As I turned into the alley to go back upstairs a cop stopped me. It seems that the folks in the car that I said something to were members of the neighborhood watch team. They happened to pass a cop along Market Street and told him that some nut was out on Tenth Street making threatening gestures at them. I told the cop what had happened, but he didn't seem to care. He told me to come down to the police station with him. I was only a block away from the police station so I said, "Okay." He knew who I was so he allowed me to walk down. When I got there he wanted to lock me up for the night but I told him to let go home because my wife and son were home alone without a way to secure our front door because of the break-in. He ignored me and continued filling out his report. I was ready to walk out when the neighborhood watch people came into the station. They didn't want to talk to me until I told them who I was. One of them knew the Penn's Port Websters so they lighten up a little. By the time I was done talking to them, they wanted me to join their group and ride around town with them. The cop eventually let me go. The next day, another cop came to fill out another report and witness the damage. He ended up telling me that the locks were too weak and that they would probably never catch the person responsible for breaking in.

It took me until the next day before I realized it was her little brother, Carlo that took our money. Marie knew right away who it was but decided to let me figure it out for myself. Marie and I went up to her parent's house to tell them, but no one cared. I just wanted everyone in her family to know that we thought it was their brother/son, who took his sisters and nephew's rent money. As time passed nothing else was said about the missing money.

The boys in her family continued to get into trouble a lot. It seemed to me that desperation and excitement got in the way of common sense and honor. Another time I took her second younger brother Angelo to court. He got caught stealing a television from a T.V. repair shop in Penn's Port and when the cop showed up, he threw the T.V. at the cop and ran. I remember the judge asked how he pled to the charges of burglary and assaulting an officer. Angelo's public defender said "Nolo Contenda." Angelo turned to me and said, "What the fuck is that?" I just said," I don't know but just stay quiet." The judge fined him and put him on probation. ✎

# Chapter 17: Steady Job

Marie began working with her mother at the Salvation Army store in Penn's Port and, in September of 1976, I got a job at nearby Congore Corporation. They made vinyl floor covering. I was able to land this job because Marie knew a lady at the bank that knew someone at Congore who could help me get hired. This was a very good event. I was really glad to get this job. Congore was on my "B" list as one of the most desirable places to work in the area. I was going to make the best of it. I could walk to work if I wanted to. Coincidently, my brother James got a job there two days earlier. His girlfriend's father worked there and recommended James for the job. We both worked in the shipping department. I thought we had it made. The pay was a cut above minimum wage and we received good health benefits and to me, it wasn't hard work. Everybody except the foreman had to work different shifts. We worked three weeks on each shift. On second and third shifts when our assignments were completed we didn't have to do anything except hang out in the back and drink alcohol and play cards. We used to call the place "The Congo" because of all the Blacks that worked there. The shipping department was about seventy percent African American. Everyone there got along pretty well because we had a consistency of purpose. All an employee had to do was come to work every day and finish their assignments. The bosses would set the teams so we would team up and load a couple of trucks and, when finished, we would go back to where the other people of your same race hung out and wait for the shift to end.

On the home front; one day I came home from work and Fredrico was there hanging out with Marie. Fredrico asked me if I wanted to meet my new neighbors. The apartment next door had been vacant for a while so when someone moved in it was news. I thought that it was nice of him to meet my neighbors for me. He then handed me some Instamatic photos of a young couple about my age posing nude and in sexually suggestive positions. I asked him where he got them and Marie answered me by saying; "He went into their apartment and snooped around into their personal stuff and came back with those." I handed them back to him and asked him to put them back but, of course, he kept the photos for himself.

The Volpes didn't do crimes around me most of the time. They had special friends for that. But I could have been caught up with their misdeeds at any given time. For instance, I looked in my refrigerator's freezer one time and found small packets of drugs. I asked Marie what it was and she said, "Carlo asked me if he could use our refrigerator to hold his stuff. I told him that you weren't going to like it, but he left it there anyway." I was really disappointed in her for not having the strength to tell him, no. Carlo and I never did get along very well. Even before the missing rent money, I had a bad feeling about this kid brother of hers. I asked her how she would like it if a dope fiend found out about him leaving drugs in our apartment and decided to break in to get the drugs. Marie didn't say anything. I just told her to tell him to get his stuff and not to use our place for stashing drugs anymore.

Another time, on a Saturday night, the usual crew, Fredrico, Popeye, Samuel and I were relaxing and drinking up at her mom's house until we ran out of beer. We decide to go out and get some more. Samuel asked me for a ride down to Penn's Port to get it. The time was around 10 p.m. and, for some reason, everyone wanted to go. I drove with Fredrico sitting in the front and Samuel and Carlo in the backseat. We went down to Penn's Port and instead of going to a bar, Fredrico wanted to hang a right on Tenth Street and drive towards Delaware. I did and after a block of passing my apartment, there were no more businesses, residences or any place to buy beer. Sun Oil was on either side of the road until you reached the state of Delaware. Sammy said, "Pull over. I got to take a piss." As I did, I noticed these guys walking on the other side of the street heading in the opposite direction. They must have been foreign merchant marines returning to their ship, after a shopping spree in Delaware. We saw them around town all the time and some people preyed on them. All of a sudden, everyone, except me, got out of the car and started to assault the men. There were five foreigners and just three Volpes and me. I just sat there in the driver's seat trying not to get involved. I looked across the street and saw Fredrico standing over this guy, he was submitting by taking off his watch to give to Fredrico and pleading for mercy. Another two victims were climbing over the fence to flee into the refinery to get away from the danger. I couldn't see what Carlo was doing, but Samuel took off his belt and was swinging at one of them. He took a swing at him and struck the man with the buckle but only slightly hurt him so the guy got up and started to run from his attacker. Samuel chased him but couldn't reach the poor guy. The victim used my car to keep it between him and Samuel to avoid a beating. As he ran to the front of my car, Samuel yelled, "Run him over, Run him over." I just sat doing nothing; like the nobody that I am. Within three minutes, the mayhem is over and my brothers in law got back in the car. They were all exhausted from the physical outburst and excitement. I dropped them off and went to my apartment just about a quarter-mile from the incident. The next day, I was scared that one of the victims would recognize my car from the night before. It was Sunday and the Quaker Market was closed so I parked my car in their lot so it would be out of site from Tenth Street. The next Monday I asked Marie to find out if anyone coming into the Salvation Army Store talked about what happened. She said one customer said something about some "niggers" jumping sailors off the boats. I never heard anything more about it.

The Webster's were doing all right for themselves. Elizabeth was still teaching school. By then she became a Mother Superior. The order of nuns she belonged to lightened up on the outfits. They shortened the black dress to four inches below the knee and the veil and bonnet softened up, too. It was now just a black cloth with a white headband. Their hair was exposed to show some color and texture. Ann stopped dating Petie and married this guy we called "Hairy" and they moved down to Delaware. Holly and Chrissy stayed with my parents. My third sister, Kathy, moved into a house with her husband, Wayne, and they had a baby girl they named Donna. Jimmy rented a house with his girlfriend and their little girl, Summer. John was still in the army stationed in Hawaii. Gerald was recently discharged from the service and living at home with our younger siblings. He would come down and visit sometimes with whatever girl he was dating. Mary was dating a disco dancer named George from South Philly. Joan started a serious relationship with Bobby Truitt's brother, Ronnie. Kevin and Ruth were doing fine. Dad was doing well and Mom kept trying to tell me about little Phillie's "id" - whatever that is.

Jimmy and I joined the same softball team. People around there took their softball seriously. They had bar teams and firehouse teams. He joined a firehouse team and I asked if I could join. I had to become a contributing member first before joining the team. We had a good time. I knew I could hit at least one home run every game and at first, I thought I was too good to play softball with a bunch of fat drunks. I was soon to find out that there were enough teams with pretty good athletes that could also hit a home run every game. Pretty soon I accepted hitting around .400 averages as the norm so it ended up being fun. It was also a chance for me to be around another type of people for a while.

In February 1977, Marie was pregnant again. I was still working at Congore and things were looking up for us. One morning we woke up to find Driftwood School had burnt down. We went up to her mother's house to take a look. While standing in their backyard, we could see across the playground to the extensive damage caused by the fire. The police and fire officials were looking around the completely destroyed building. How could this happen? Driftwood's number one firehouse is less than two hundred yards away from the school. And Driftwood's number two firehouse is only about three hundred yards away from that. A few of Marie's family members were in their back yard with us. When her youngest brother Joey came near me, I noticed he smelled of gasoline and, he had a burnt pant leg.

Narrow-minded me said, "Joey, how did you do that to your pant leg?"

He says, "I accidentally spilled some lighter fluid on my pants and, when I fell asleep with a cigarette, it caught my pant leg on fire."

I said, "You better go upstairs and change your pants before the cops think you might have had something to do with the fire last night."

Marie's fifteen-year-old brother Joey said, "They better not come over here without a warrant because we can shoot them for trespassing."

The next day, Joey was arrested with two other boys from Driftwood and eventually convicted of arson and ordered to pay retribution and sent to a boy's home in upstate Pennsylvania for a year and a half.

Marie found a two-story, three-bedroom, semi-detached home in Driftwood for rent and that spring we moved in. It wasn't long before her family started coming over on the weekends. I didn't mind that much. They were all right people most of the time. Carlo would come in with his brothers sometimes, but we still didn't like each other. One night, Popeye and I were playing cards in the kitchen while Fredrico, Carlo, and Samuel were in the front room with Marie. Carlo was trying to get Marie to sign a piece of paper saying he lived with us and paid rent. That way he could go to the welfare office and tell them he needed money to pay his rent and get some free money. Of course, she said, no the first four times he asked. He started to get angry with her and started saying, "You think you are so good now, you can't even help your own brother. Oh, Miss Goodie Two Shoes thinks she is better than everyone else. We all know the things she used to do." Well, this really pissed me off. Earlier, I was sitting in the kitchen listening and waiting for one of her older brothers to stand up for their sister, but they never did. I went in there and told him that I was going to stop him from using our address even if she did sign the paper. I would call the welfare office and tell them the truth. Besides that, if he was going to talk to his sister in that manner he was going to have to leave. That brother of hers was giving me stomach pains. Just thinking about him sent an adrenaline rush in my belly. If I ever developed an ulcer I was going to name it," Carlo." ∽

## Chapter 18: Isn't She Lovely

In August 1977, Jennifer Webster was born. Marie was induced into labor for eight hours and I was allowed to see her give birth. Everything came out just perfect. Marie was in the pre-delivery room and, while waiting, the doctor and I watched a Phillies doubleheader baseball game. Seeing a live birth is one of those things that is beautiful to see. If I describe it in writing, I just couldn't do it justice. She was a beautiful little girl, 8 pounds, 4 ounces. After Marie and Jennifer came home from the hospital my mom came over and cooked us a roast beef dinner.

Work was going well and I got to hang around with James during the time our shifts met. I was still doing stupid stuff after our assignments were completed. I would sneak out the back door and cross the railroad tracks and go to a bar to buy some beer and sneak it back into work. I am sad to say that I did this. I must have been out of my mind to jeopardize my job like that.

Soon after Marie had Jennifer, I developed a pilonidal cyst on the base of my spine and it would not heal. I needed surgery to remove it. I went into the hospital for three days and that's when I found out about good drugs. The doctor prescribed Demerol for the pain. The only way I can describe it is by saying it made you feel very, very smooth. I was feeling no pain and having great conversations with people that weren't even in the room. I wanted more and more, but the night nurse refused by saying that the doctor only allowed three doses and I already had them. She offered me a massage instead and I said, "No thank you."

The winter of 1977-1978 came and it was bad. The snow was deeper than it had been for the last ten years. All the roads were closed, including where I worked, so I shoveled my sidewalk and went to my mom and dad's to shovel theirs. Gerald had already started so I helped him finish and when I was done, I went over to the Howard's house to clear a path on their sidewalk. Timmy Howard was attending a cooking school in Arizona with his sisters and his mother was living alone now, so I decided to do her a favor.

I saw my old friends very rarely, but I did ask about them if I ran across one of them. Gunther Price got the DeMarco's older sister pregnant and had to marry her. Dave Rose had long broken up with my sister, Mary, and was now in and out of the Marines. He later became a guard at the county jail. Carmine and Danny DeMarco were in a severe car accident, the kind where no one knows who was actually driving the car. Carmine came out of intensive care long before Danny. Danny received permanent brain damage and he was never the same. I heard that my friend Petie Pillsbury moved to New York and turned into a heavy drinker and KW smoker, (KW is short for Killer Weed, which is parsley soaked in chemicals like formaldehyde and jet fuel and other toxic ingredients that bring the smoker to a place where only insane people reside.)

One night, around eleven p.m., Marie and I heard a commotion on our front porch. We looked out of our front bedroom window to see what the hell all the ruckus was about. We recognized her brother Angelo so when he knocked on the door Marie went down to answer it. Two years earlier he got Wally Storms younger sister pregnant. They had a son, baby Angelo. Marie was talking loudly to her brother saying you can't do that. I decided to go down to see what was going on. It seems Angelo took his baby's mother out to the wooded area near the little league baseball field to beat the crap out of her. Every time he hit her the child started to scream and cry.

As I got to the door, Marie stepped aside and she said, "Phillip talk to him for me."

I asked, "What's going on?"

He said, "Every time I hit her, the baby starts screaming and crying so I need you guys to watch him for me until I get back."

As he finished his last word he handed the child to Marie and started to drag his girlfriend kicking and screaming off our porch. I looked to see her hanging on for dear life. Her desperation was obvious so I stepped outside to tell him to let her go. I told him that someone around here would call the cops if they didn't shut up and come inside. We went in to talk about the problem. After having some tea and changing the subject they relaxed enough to leave without him hurting her. At least Gale and the baby were safe for that night.

In April of 1978, Mrs. Howard called my mom and said, "Because Phillip was so nice and shoveled the snow from my sidewalk without anyone asking him to and without asking for anything in return, and since my bungalow is vacant, he can move in there with his wife and kids if he wants." It was one of four detached houses with two bedrooms, a front porch and a small back yard along Claremont St. The rent was only $110 a month. We moved in right away. We lost the deposit from the Huddle Street house, but we didn't have to give Mrs. Howard any deposit before moving into her place. Our new address was Claremont Street, Driftwood, PA.

As far as I was concerned, we just hit the jackpot. I was bringing home $147.00 a week in pay. I felt comfortable living just two houses up the street from my Mom and Dad. It wasn't Marie's favorite place to live but it suited me just fine. Phillie was just about to turn four years old in June and he was starting to enjoy hanging around with his cousin Chrissy. Chrissy was really a sweet child. At three months old, she had open-heart surgery and we all felt bad for her. Her father hardly came around but, just like Holly, we all treated her like a sister. Marie's nephew, little Mattie, came by to visit which was fine with me. Jennifer was seven months old and getting prettier every day. We were lucky to have two very healthy children. Our children could have had all of our bad features, but they didn't. They had all of Marie and my best looks.

Next door was Mrs. Howard who lived alone most of the time. Her brothers, the priests, came by most weekends. They let us

Websters call them Uncle instead of Father just as if we were related to them. Uncle Norm was all right but snooped around a lot. Marie swore that sometimes he would come up on our porch and peek into our bedroom. I did hear him out there one Saturday morning but he was just trimming the rose bushes that started to climb up our front porch railing. He loved those bushes and I'd seen him take very good care of those flowers for years. Uncle Charles was hardly noticeable; I don't think he gave a shit about the roses. He would just sit in his backyard reading a book.

Marie's three younger sisters, Silvia, Olivia, and Monica, stopped coming over as much. Olivia started to go up to her brother Anthony's and spent her free time there. When we finally did see her she looked as if she might be pregnant. Occasionally, on the weekends, her brothers came over to party, but that was about it. This was considered my neighborhood. Popeye liked to come by with his friend Ralph to watch Saturday Night Live and smoke pot.

One early Sunday morning, Marie and I were sleeping in late when we heard a disturbance on our front porch. It's was her old man and her brother Joey breaking into our house. We hardly locked the door since we moved to Claremont Street. I usually just put a latch on the screen door. Well, they went right through it and walked into our bedroom looking around our bed when the old man asked us, "Where is Silvia?"

I jumped up and asked, "Why are you here?"

He repeated, "I want to know where Silvia is?"

I was stunned by these accusations. Did he really think Silvia would be in our bedroom while I was in there? Marie got up as they went out of our bedroom and towards our kids' room.

The old man was saying, "I know she's in here."

Marie said, "She isn't here and hasn't been here since Friday. She stopped by after school and she went to a friend's house."

This really bothered Marie a lot more than it bothered me. I thought it was very rude, but the guy is a maniac when it comes to his daughters. Silvia did come over that previous Friday. She was very upset about something. I asked Marie what was going on and she said that her dad was after Silvia because she was receiving phone calls from an older guy. Marie went on to say that Silvia was now going out to meet this guy in spite of what the old man thought. I didn't think much about it because Silvia was about to turn eighteen and was, as far as I was concerned, a very good and obedient girl. Because she didn't follow the rules of a tyrant didn't bother me.

The next weekend Popeye and his sidekick, Ralph, came over to our house to hang out, listen to music, and smoke pot. We did this a lot. We liked to just sit around and listen to Pink Floyd's, "Dark Side of the Moon." As the night progressed, Marie started to act very strangely. After midnight, Popeye and Ralph left. Marie started to accuse me of having intimate eye contact with Ralph.

I said, "What the hell are you talking about?"

She said in a very defiant way, "I saw you. Don't try to get out of it. You and Ralph were giving each other the eye."

"Marie, what are you talking about?"

She said, "I saw the way you two looked at each other, giving each other the eye and thinking no one was going to see you."

This was starting to get way out of line. It was getting late and I wanted to end this conversation before it got out of hand. There were times when we would fight and most of the time I don't know what caused it. This time there was no earthly reason for us to do battle tonight, especially as bizarre as this conversation was becoming.

The kids were already in bed, so I said, "Let's hit the sack and talk about it in the morning."

She said in a manner as if I was some stranger, "Go in there by yourself, I'm staying out here."

I went to put my arm around her and she said very defiantly, "Don't you put your dirty hands on me."

I said, "Marie you need some rest, please just come to bed."

She said in a way that meant she wasn't going to do anything that would make me happy, "You would like that, wouldn't you?"

She said, "Keep away from me," as she lay down on the dining room floor near the washing machine. She curled herself up in a near fetal position and started to sob. I was very confused and started to worry, but I didn't want to make a scene and wake up the kids. I went into our bedroom hoping she would soon follow. I left the door open so I could see her. I could only see the bottom of her feet from where I was laying. It was late and I was tired. I fell asleep hoping to wake up the next morning to find Marie lying next to me recovered from this spell she was under.

Shortly after I was able to get into a sound sleep, I was awakened by a noise coming from the dining room. Marie started to moan and make mumbling noises with her voice that came from a deep and dark place inside of her tormented past; the place where good and evil fight for control of your soul. I started to get scared. I went into the hallway that separated the kid's room from the rest of the house. I just wanted to know if I could still hear my wife because I didn't want our children to hear this sound coming from their mother. I walked into the dining room to be next to her. I sat beside her, pleading with her to come to our bedroom so we could talk about her problems.

She said, "I know that you and your brother John are faggots."

I said, "What the hell does my brother, John's sexuality have to do with any of this?"

I didn't want to fathom why she thought I was a homosexual. There was no reaching her. She was in a place that I had never experienced dealing with. I stayed between Marie and Phillie's and Jenny's bedroom, sitting on the floor, staying awake all night. Keeping myself close enough to her to be there for her if she needed me, and not too close to cause her any discomfort.

Daylight finally came and I said, "Marie please get up, someone might come over to see you like this."

She got up, and went into the bedroom and immediately shut the door. I took the hint and didn't follow her. I could hear Jenny crying so I went into the kid's room to see what she was crying about. She needed her bottle refreshed and her diaper changed. She was going to turn one-year-old in a week and was already starting to walk. I cleaned her up and placed her in her playpen that was located in the living room. Jenny usually spent most of the day either in her playpen or in her spring-suspended "bouncy" chair. Phillie woke up during this time and asked for his mother. I told him she wasn't feeling very well. Phillie and I went into the kitchen to get a bowl of cereal. Marie came out of the room. Marie must have heard what I said to Phillie.

She came out and said, "Oh, you would like that wouldn't you?"

I asked, "What do you mean?"

She said, "You would like to get rid of me, wouldn't you?"

I said, "Of course not, and you know that."

I decided not to talk to her anymore and hoped things would settle down. Marie spent the day taking care of the kids and lying on the couch. I spent the day staying at least one room apart from her. I sat out on the front porch for the entire morning wondering what to do. No one from her family came over that day and we didn't go over to have Sunday dinner with them. It was as if her family had sensed something was wrong. As night fell, things got worse. She went into the same area of the dining room as the night before, this time right on top of a pile of dirty clothes and started to sob again. She pulled articles of cloths over her even though it was a very hot August night. The fear and pain were audible. I tried softly calling her name, but I couldn't make contact with her. It was as if she was another person. My wife had become a mean and disturbed being.

I said, "Marie, what has a hold of you? Please talk to me. I am your husband and tell me what is hurting you so much. I won't let anyone hurt you. No one can bother you now, because you are with me. Please trust me I will do anything to help you. I do not fear anyone when it comes to protecting my family. You know that, Marie. Do you want me to go get your dad to help you?"

She said, "No!"

It was a very definite no. She started to mumble some things about him and the devil, but she was still barely audible. This continued through the evening. I needed some help with her this time and it was too late for me to be too embarrassed to tell someone in my family what was going on.

It was past one in the morning when Marie got up and said, "I have to get out of here." She stood up and walked towards the door. I pleaded with her not to go but she ran out the door and up the street anyhow. I started to follow her. She was crying out loud as she was heading towards her parent's house but instead of going to the end of Claremont Street and turning right, she turned left before she got to the corner of Claremont and Huddle Street and ran up Hooper Drive. I followed her and caught her. I begged her to come back home, saying we shouldn't leave the kids alone for very long.

She stopped and asked, "How much money do we have in the bank?" I said we have enough to get by for now. She said she wanted money, so she and her sister Silvia could go away together.

I asked, "Why, Marie, haven't I've been good to you?'

She didn't answer me. I took my chance and said the banks aren't open until after 9 a.m. tomorrow so why don't you come back to the house and get some rest. To my relief, Marie complied and slept on the couch. I stayed up again most of the night and the next morning, I called my work and told them I was sick and would not be coming in today. I let Marie sleep, hoping that she would sleep right through the day but she got up around ten o'clock. She was determined to go and run away with her younger sister, Silvia. Because my wife didn't have any proper identification, I tried to foil her attempt to get the money out of the bank by not going with her.

But she started to get upset again and said, "I will go out and get the money somehow, so you might as well let me have it now."

I asked her where she was going and where was she going to stay.

She said, "I don't care where I go. Maybe I'll take Silvia on a bus to Delaware."

I asked, "What about the kids?" Marie said she would come back to get them as soon as she got settled.

I wrote her a personal check for two hundred and fifty-dollars and off she went. As soon as she left, I called her mom at the Salvation Army Store in Penn's Port. Marie and I started a bank account at the Philadelphia National Bank, the same bank where Marie knew the lady that helped me get a job at Congore. It was right down the street from where her mom worked. I told her mom how upset Marie had become and what her plans were. Mrs. Volpe said that she was going to call her husband to go and get her because he knew how to handle things like this. I said that it is not a good idea, because Marie was saying some bad things about her father while she was having a nightmare. Her mom said, "That's alright, he'll know what to do." In the pit of my stomach, I knew this was a bad idea. I hung up the phone and called my mother and asked her to come over to talk with me. As I saw my mom coming up to the front porch, I broke down and cried like a baby. I was twenty-four years old and sobbed uncontrollably. I had had enough and couldn't take any more heartache. I told my mom of the horror that we went through the last two days and nights.

Mom recognized Marie's condition and asked where the kids were. I said, "Jenny is taking a nap in her playpen and Phillie is in their room playing." I told my mom that Marie went down to Penn's Port to get money out of the bank so she and Silvia could take a bus to Delaware. It seemed like a couple of minutes later when her old man showed up.

He came to the house and said, "Marie wants her kids to be with her."

I said, "Where is she?"

He said, "She is over at the house and she will be just fine in a couple of days."

I asked, "Are you sure? She was very upset the entire weekend."

He didn't stop to talk. He collected my children and went out the door.

As he was leaving my mom said, "Mr. Volpe, I think Marie may need professional help."

He said, "I don't think so, we've never had any lulus in our family."

He actually paused and said, "Except for my sister's husband Paulie."

I could not believe he said that. My wife and children were in the hands of a man that thinks people with mental/emotional problems are lulus.

In a matter of three days, my whole life came crumbling down and I couldn't figure out what to do about it.

About two o'clock in the afternoon, I called her house and asked to speak to Marie, but when she got on the phone she said that she didn't want to talk to me.

This hurt me, but I said, "Can I call you later?"

She said, "If you want."

I called back two hours later. I sensed a change in the tone of her voice this time and it gave me a glimmer of hope.

I said, "Can we go for a ride to get some fresh air and I will bring you right back?" She said, "Okay."

I drove over to pick her up and we went for a ride out past Upper Manchester. People had small farms with horses out there. Sometimes, when we wanted to get away from all the noise and commotion we would drive out there. This day we found a secluded spot far away from any houses and I parked the car. It was a mid-August Monday afternoon and no one was around.

We started to take a walk in an open field. I tried to convince her that the best place for her and our children was with me. Deep down in her soul, she knew this to be true. I am not very smart, so I didn't have a clue what we were going to do but I knew if we stayed together, it would all work out. I also knew that I had to convince her that her family didn't scare me. They could not control me with fear. If she would only trust me to do the right thing, they could not touch her. I let her know that no matter what else happened I was not going to let her family raise my kids. I told her what my mom said to him and about the "lu-lu" statement the old man had said in front of me and my mom. I told her what a fucking nut he was and that normal everyday people don't speak like that when it comes down to serious problems. With that, she finally started to loosen up. Marie finally settled down and was able to tell me what was going on.

Marie said, "Her father would come into her younger sister's bedroom at night and force Silvia to have sex with him." Only these poor girls really knew what happened those times when he satisfied his dirty and selfish requests. Marie continued to say that was why Silvia wanted to run away a week earlier. Marie also admitted to me that he was the man in the car that molested her when she was six years old. She said she ran away from home because her father was beating her brother so bad she could not stand it anymore. I was devastated by this revelation; I didn't want her to say any more about the issue.

All that I said was, "Do you want me to kill him for you? Tomorrow morning I will wait for him to get in his car and I will cut his throat."

I was thinking of using a very capable butcher knife I found behind the Quaker Meat Market. One forceful slice will do the job. Right after I said that I wanted to recall every word. I started to think of the details like hiding in the bushes separating their property from their neighbors. I would have to disengage his car's horn so he couldn't blow it as his vile life's blood left his wicked body. I also wondered if I had the nerve to kill this Incestuous Zombie.

Marie said, "No! Let's just get the kids and go far, far away from here and never look back."

I said, "Okay, that's what we will do."

We drove back to her parent's house to pick up Phillie and Jenny and told everyone that things were back to normal now and we were going home. That night I lay in bed restlessly, but Marie was able to rest peacefully for the first time in three days. We decided not to tell anyone in her family about our plans to leave them. I went to work the next day and put in my voluntary separation two weeks' notice. I asked my mom if she thought it would be a good idea for us to go to California, near her cousin Jimmy Doyle. I had eight hundred dollars in the savings account and waited a couple of days to take it all out. I didn't have car insurance, so I went to an Auto Insurance agency to get some. Since I was going to drive across the country, I might need it. My car was in good enough shape to do the job, so long as I didn't turn corners or accelerate too quickly. It just needed a tune-up before we started our journey.

Three days past and I was getting excited about the move. Marie wanted to say goodbye to her brothers and sisters and nieces and nephews before we took off. We went over to their house the next day and made the announcement. I was very anxious about the trip but didn't say anything to anyone. I asked Marie's brother, Fredrico to help me tune up the car like he had a few times before. I drove the car down to the Mall to get spark plugs, four cans of oil, and oil and gas filters. Fredrico said he would take care of it for me. When he got done the car wouldn't start. I tried to start the car while he adjusted the carburetor and that usually worked, but not this time. I don't know what happened exactly, but the piece of shit just wouldn't start.

I didn't skip a beat. I went up to Castleton and paid $75 apiece for two Greyhound bus tickets for San Francisco, California. We were leaving the next evening. Everyone in both families was surprised by these sudden events. No one in my family asked why we decided to leave so suddenly and I didn't tell them. I guess my Mom knew what was really going on, but never said a word.

I remember my father who hardly ever said a word about anything or anybody came over to my house the day we were leaving and said, "Phillip, when you go out to California you might have to live next door to Mexicans or colored people."

I said, "Okay dad, I will be fine."

We collected a few items, mostly summer and spring clothes, and put them in two large suitcases and grabbed Marie's purse and Jenny's diaper bag and walked out the door. I didn't care about the furniture or any other material things remaining in the house. What did bother me was the look on little Chrisy's face when she said goodbye to her cousin Phillie, boy oh boy that look on her face made me feel terrible. And, for some reason, my sister Katherine started to cry. That surprised me a bit. I don't know why, but it did. ∽

# Chapter 19: A Bus Ride From Hell

We boarded the bus in Castleton and left the driving to them. The first bus we boarded was crowded but we were only going to Philadelphia to get a transfer to Pittsburg. We were taking the northern route across the country. We had to wait for a couple of hours in Philly, but at least we were on our way. There were a lot of rough-looking characters around.

I started to remember what Marie's brother, Matthew, said when Samuel started that fight with the Heathens. Since we both lived in Penn's Port at the time, I worried about what might happen when we crossed paths with some of the club members. I asked if he was afraid of the Heathens we might have to go up against. His reply was, once you turn twenty-years-old and weigh close to two hundred pounds, there aren't too many people in this world that scare you. I had physically matured steadily until age twenty-four. I was six foot two and 1/2 inches tall and one hundred and eighty-five pounds and a good athlete. I still carried that air of confidence that allowed me to get through most predicaments. And, if all else failed, I carried that capable butcher knife tucked down the back of my pants' waistband. I felt as though I could handle myself well enough to protect my family and make it across the country.

My biggest fear had passed. Marie was back with me and trying to start a new life, away from her family's control. If anything happened to my kids like if somebody in her family molested Phillie or Jennifer, it would be too late to do anything. Even if I killed them all, my children would have been molested and scarred for the rest of their lives.

I was carrying my life's saving with me and only a few people knew this. I separated the cash in three places. After spending money on the car and bus tickets and leaving some in the checking account to cover the checks we wrote, I had six hundred dollars for the trip. Fifty-dollars in my pants front pocket, one hundred and fifty dollars in my wallet, and the rest in a billfold stuck down the front of my pants.

We boarded the bus for Pittsburg late, around midnight, and rode through the night. A couple of Black guys stuck out to me. I figured that they were just "gritting" on me. They were sizing me up because that's what these types of guys do to everyone. The ride through Pennsylvania was nerve-racking. Someone put an empty glass bottle in the aisle and it rolled back and forth all night long. The driver was speeding up and down the Allegany Mountains like he was having fun. Just when I was about to throw up, he pulled over. This caused one of the Black guys that I noticed gritting on me earlier to wake up and the first thing he did was to look back at me as if to see if I was still there. This bothered me a little, but I couldn't figure out what his problem was. He wasn't a big guy but it seemed to me that he was from somewhere deep in the ghetto. He wore a white sleeveless wife-beater t-shirt and pair of copper fluorescent dress pants. All he carried was a towel around his neck and a toothbrush in his back pocket. His partner was a little bigger than he but not as threatening because he didn't seem as interested in us.

The driver waited until daybreak before pulling into downtown Pittsburg. We collected everything we carried on and exited the bus. We went into the bus station restaurant and had breakfast. Phillie and Jenny behaved themselves like angels, no fussing or complaints at all. God only knows what was going through their heads. Phillie was four and Jenny was about to have her first birthday. I was so mixed up; I didn't even know what day it was. Marie's instincts took over. She sat there and talked to the kids and kept them busy with coloring books and playing paddy cake and things like that. We traveled with either Jenny or Phillie on one of our laps. As we were about to re-enter the bus for the next leg of the journey, I stopped by a trashcan because I needed to throw Jenny's dirty diaper away. The guys that were interested in us were standing next to the trashcan with their boom box radio sitting on the lid. I had to walk past them to dispose of our trash. I figured if they were going to say something to me this would be the best time since I was by myself. I just looked at them and said, "Excuse me," before I reached passed them. They ignored me as I got rid of our trash. The next leg of the trip was from Pittsburgh to Cleveland.

We re-boarded the bus to travel to Cleveland. We sat on the driver's side about mid-way between the front and back. I was exhausted by now and could not stay awake. The same two guys as before got on our bus and this time I noticed a third person had joined them. As each one passed, he gave me a dirty look. The entire passenger list was a motley crew, including us. It reminded me of when I stood in the welfare line. The one guy with the copper pants started to talk trash out loud. He was about four rows behind us but made sure everyone around heard him as he talked bad about White people. I couldn't understand all of what he was saying, so I looked around because I knew a young White girl was riding in a seat behind us. The look on her face said it all. She was very afraid. I could not help myself and I fell asleep.

What seemed like a second later, Marie woke me up by elbowing me in the side.

She said, "Those guys back there are talking about us."

I said, "What guys are you talking about?"

She said, "Those Black guys that rode with us from Philadelphia. They knew everything about us. They know our names, where we are going, and the fact that we have a lot of money with us."

I thought, Oh no! My worst nightmare is coming true. I stopped to listen and now they were only two seats behind us. He was running his mouth, spouting out crap about me. He said that I was a blue-eyed devil. He said I was a Nazi and that I thought I was good with my hands, but he could out-box me. He was going to open me up and cut my guts out, and take my eight hundred dollars. He said we were never going to make it to California. When he said that no one cared what happened to me or my kids, I could not believe my ears. Again, I looked around to see if any of the other passengers heard what was going on. They all had this blank look on their faces as if they didn't care what was going on, or that they were glad it wasn't them. I was on my own with this new obstacle.

The bus finally made it into the Cleveland depot. Marie asked what we were going to do.

My thought of him hurting me only progressed to the point of imminent physical injury; at that point, my thoughts rapidly turned to me hurting him. All that I needed was for him to make the first move, then I could justify in my mind the need to get physical. His verbal threats weren't enough for me to thrust my knife into his neck.

I said to Marie, "First, let everyone else get off the bus. We need to be sure to gather our thoughts and all our stuff together before we get off the bus."

I looked up and saw as the young White girl exiting the bus giving me a similar look that Marie gave me years before while I was sitting in her kitchen talking to her brother about the shooting. A compassioned look that said, "You're in deep shit boy." I looked at her like, "You know what's going on, don't you? But don't worry about me girl, look out for yourself."

It seemed like seconds when everyone was off the bus and we needed to get off ourselves. The one big mouth guy was standing at the end of the aisle just before the driver's seat. His original backup was standing inside the bus at the top of the steps and the third one was standing outside the bus blocking the entrance. They had cut my fight or flight options in half. I stood up and asked Marie to hold Jennifer and keep Phillie behind her. I placed Jenny's diaper bag strap around my neck and put the bag in front of my stomach and said a prayer. I said, "God, please don't make me kill this man today." I didn't want to have to kill anyone but I felt as if I was going to. I checked to make sure I could grab the knife quickly and started towards them. As I got within two steps of him I am sure he could see my determination. We looked at each other as if to say; one of us is going to die right here and right now if he didn't back off. All I could think of is thrusting my knife into his neck.

Marie said in a much-panicked mode, "What are you going to do to us?"

I said, "These fucking bastards aren't going to do a fucking thing."

With that, he stepped aside and the others followed suit. They crumbled like the walls of Jericho.

The first guy stepped back to the driver seat and as we passed he said, "If we don't get you here we will get you in Detroit or Chicago."

The other two moved out and away from the steps and exit. As I passed each one of them, I gave them each the same look. The look said, "Are you willing to die today because I am willing to kill you today."

Lucky for us there was a Cleveland police sub-station right inside the bus depot. I walked in and told the sergeant what just happened.

He questioned, "Why would someone pick you out to assault?"

I showed him the money I had stuffed in my billfold and he asked, "How did they know it was there?"

I said, "I don't know, but they did."

He asked, "Are the guys that did this still around?"

And then he asked me if I could pick them out for him. I said maybe, but I didn't know where they went after we passed them. The cop was alone but he was a big man about six-foot-six inches tall and two hundred and fifty pounds.

He stated, "Stay here while I go out to look around."

When he returned, he asked, "What do you want to do?"

I said, "Get away from those guys that have been after us since Philadelphia."

He asked me if I wanted to return home and I said, "No!"

After asking where we were going, he said, "How about if you take the southern route to California."

I said, "Alright as long as they could not follow us."

He said he would wait until everyone else except us boarded the southbound bus, we could get on and he would make sure nobody else boarded. I liked this idea. It felt good to have someone calm and collected in my corner, even if it was temporary.

The police officer asked the bus people to change our tickets and with his assistance, we boarded the next southbound bus. We were now heading for Indianapolis, Indiana, and on to St. Louis. I was now very paranoid and extremely exhausted. In spite of being weary I could see that we were with a much calmer and more docile group of people. It reminded me of the unemployment line. Within a few minutes, I fell asleep. When I awoke I was surprised to see Jenny in the lap of one of the little girls sitting across the aisle from us. She was with her younger sister and her mother. The girl was about twelve-years-old and her name was Debbie. I would like to meet these people someday and thank them and explain our behavior to them. The mother told Marie she was going to San Diego to meet her husband who was in the Navy. It was a relief to be next to Black people that you could relax and talk to. Jenny was a pretty little girl with blue eyes and peach fuzz blonde hair on a nicely shaped head. This pleased the little girl playing with her. Phillie was this handsome little boy with big brown eyes and a big forehead and brown curly hair. Every time we stopped Marie and I would take turns going to the bathroom, washing up the kids, and changing Jenny's diaper. Poor little Phillie, I felt bad for him having to go through this at such a young age but these young girls next to us treated him very nicely. He was wonderful though it all.

When we stopped in the big city depots, I had this air of suspicion about everyone I crossed paths with. While we were in St. Louis, an incident happened that bothered me. The mother of the girls that were holding Jenny was standing in the bus station common area.

I was in the men's room when this Black guy said, "How are you doing?"

He said this while we were standing in the bathroom washing our hands. Typically men don't talk to each other while they are in the men's room.

I responded by saying, "I'm alright, how are you?"

And when he asked where I was from. I got really nervous. I just paused and looked at him as if to say, why are you asking me this?

He said, "Are you from the east coast?"

I said, "Yea."

As I finished washing and drying my hands, he said, "Are you from New York?"

I said, "Yes."

I turned and left the bathroom puzzled by this encounter.

When I got near Marie I heard this older Negro woman saying angrily to Debbie's mother. "Why are you holding that White child? Are you her Mammy or what?" I felt bad for the lady trying to do us a favor and holding Jennifer.

I asked if she wanted me to take her and she said in a dignified manner, "No, I have her. She will be fine with me."

I believed her, she was a strong and independent woman who wasn't going to let someone tell her who she could or couldn't be nice to.

We got back on the bus and continued on our way. I fell into a deep sleep and had a dream as real as life itself. Marie's father was walking down the bus aisle towards me. Just as he was about to reach me, I woke up. I've never had a dream as real as that was, before or since. I remember seeing the signs for Joplin, Missouri and thinking, "What if we got off the bus at the next stop would we be able to start a new life?" I looked out the window of the bus and imagined myself finding work around here. I didn't see much of anything except small towns and farms. The thought slowly drifted away. Every hour, miles of road were being pushed back from under the wheels never to be seen by me again.

The next big city was Tulsa, Oklahoma. We pulled in around suppertime. We were all hungry and thankfully the little girls playing with Phillie and Jennifer had not tired with them yet. Tulsa was a typical big-city bus depot. They had a restaurant and bathroom, except the ticket office wasn't on site. It was in a separate building around the corner. Marie sat with the kids as I went to the bathroom. When I got back to where Marie was sitting, the lady and her two girls returned from where ever they went. I asked if anyone wanted something to eat and Marie said she only wanted some crackers and a soda and fresh milk for Jenny and Phillie. She said she needed to go to the bathroom and left our children with the lady and her girls. I walked through the waiting area to get soda and crackers and some food for myself but nothing seemed appetizing to me at the time.

A large panel of windows allowed you to see the parking lot, where the busses entered and cars could pull in to drop off passengers. The windows stretched the entire length of the restaurant and waiting area. I could not believe my eyes. It was that same Black guy from Cleveland. Those same ugly, copper fluorescent pants, that same white wife-beater t-shirt and the towel around his neck. He was getting out of a car with three other guys. How in the hell did he catch up with us? I was stunned. Their group got together outside their old beat-up brown Oldsmobile with the ceiling upholstery hanging down to talk or make plans or something. I froze in my tracks and couldn't decide what to do. I looked over a display of potato chips to see if Marie was aware of the situation but I couldn't see her. I saw the guys split up in groups of two and walk towards each end of the waiting area. The original guy and a partner went to the far end away from me and I passed the other two as they paused for a moment upon coming through the door nearest the restaurant. The person with him may have been the third guy in line at the Cleveland Depot but I couldn't tell for sure. The driver of the car was a big guy not quite as tall as I was but bigger-boned and heavy muscles. Wife beater shirts were also known as muscle T-shirts and this guy had every right to wear one. As I passed right next to him I noticed he had a raised scar on his left shoulder. It may have been from a bullet or something heavy like that piercing the skin. This guy was a lot tougher than the first guy. I could tell this guy wasn't going down easily. I already used up one of my three miracles to get out of the first encounter and needed another one to get out of this.

I made it to where the little girls were holding Phillie and Jenny and asked to have my kids back. They didn't want to let me have them.

The mother said, "It's okay, we don't mind. Go get something to eat, we will take care of them for you."

I said, "Please lady, you don't understand, I need to have my kids and I need them now."

Just then Marie showed up and said while clenching her teeth. "They are here and I heard them say, 'there's Webster with his two kids'."

We grabbed the kids and looked for a way out. I felt as if my imaginary trusty protective umbrella was about to collapse. Just then, I saw a janitor walk by and asked him where the offices with a phone are. Pointing to the door where the two thugs were, looking right at us, he said, "You have to go out that door, and walk around the front and across the alley to the storefront offices."

I said, "Is there another way?"

He said, "Yes! Go out the back door and walk up the alley to the main street and turn right and it is right there."

We collected our stuff and that's what we did. We opened the back door and I looked up this narrow alley that seemed a mile long. Marie was afraid to go into the alley and so was I, but I insisted that we go before they figured it out and meet us at the other end. It was scary every step of the way. I didn't know if they would come from behind us or come walking around the corner in front of us before we got to the end. But God was with us and we made it to the end of the alley and the front door of the bus ticket office. It seemed as if we made it back to civilization again. We walked inside and waited for our turn to talk to the man at the counter. The whole time I am keeping my eye on the front door.

When we finally reached the ticket man I told him what was going on. I said, like some kind of weirdo, "They are after us and they are trying to kill me."

He said, "Settle down, no one is going to harm you in here."

I said, "You don't know these people, they are determined to stop me from going to California." I went on to say, that I needed to talk to the police.

He said, "Wait right here, I will get the manager for you." As we were waiting I was still in the state of fear where your brain loses its ability to use common sense and I focused on possible threats. Courtesy went out the window when I saw a White guy and his girlfriend come into the ticket office. I felt as if he was staring at me. He reminded me of one of the punks from the west end of Castleton. I asked him what he was doing following me.

He said, "What, are you, nuts? I came in here because my girlfriend lost her bus ticket and we want to see if we could get a new one."

The manager came out and brought us back into his office and I was able to relax for a second.

He questioned, "What is your problem?" I realized how bizarre my story might sound so I told him as few details as possible. I asked him to call the police for us. I needed to report a crime.

As he called the police we waited inside the bus station office until the police arrived. The cop was a sergeant and he had a young recruit with him. The sergeant asked us what we needed from him.

I said, "Protection."

"From what?" he asked. I told him that we were next door in the bus station waiting room when a man threatened to harm my wife if she didn't go outside with him. And that he said he will be back to get her, later.

The cop asked, "Is he still around?"

I said, "He walked away when I returned."

The cop asked what he could do for us?

I said; help us get away from here.

He asked, "Do you want me to take you to the downtown YMCA, so you and your family can stay there for a couple of nights until this all passes over?"

I said, "No, I think he might have access to us there." I told him I just want to go back home from where I started.

He said, "I can take you to the Airport. You can get a ticket to wherever you want to go." The cop asked, "Do you have any money?"

After I showed him the cash I had in my pocket we all got into the back seat of his patrol car and he turned on his sirens and escorted us to the Tulsa International Airport.

We left everything on the bus except our money and Marie's purse and Jenny's diaper bag. The police sergeant escorted us to the ticket counter where we looked for the next flight to Philadelphia. When we found a flight that wasn't booked solid we bought the only tickets. I thanked the cops and we went on our way. The only tickets left were first-class fares, stopping in St. Louis and connecting to Philadelphia. The tickets cost over five hundred dollars. It was well worth the price. Someone got all my money but at least it wasn't those hoods and no one got hurt.

As we walked down the passageway towards the departure gate, Marie paused and said, "Phillip, hold up a second."

I was expecting her to say thanks for getting us through this. Instead, she said, "Are they going to check our carry-on bags before we board the plane?"

I said, "Maybe, why do you ask?"

To my astonishment, she pulled out a huge bag of Marijuana.

I said, very calmly, "Give it to me, please."

I walked over to a row of public phones. You know the ones out in the open with just a small partition between each phone. I looked around and when the coast was clear, I discreetly placed the bag of pot on top of one of the phones and walked away.

The plane ride from Tulsa to St. Louis was uneventful. We didn't smell very well, even me because my cyst was beginning to open up again. Jennifer didn't have any clean clothes and she wore a baby's undershirt and diaper. After enduring the embarrassment of knowing you don't smell or look your best on a plane that was about an hour-long, in those conditions it seemed like an eternity before we landed. We were one of the first to debark and some crazy guy ran past us while yelling back at the stewardess something about he wanted to kill himself and take everyone with him. That freaked me out again, so I told the airline employee at the exit that I wanted to talk to security. When security showed up I told him what I went through the last couple of days and why we looked as we did.

Luckily, the stewardess was still around when security gave me a curious look. I said, "Ask her if some young man was acting crazy and making threatening comments." She confirmed my story, and they took us to the VIP room to be safe while we waited for the next flight from St. Louis to Philadelphia. Marie and I talked a little and the airline employee that was assigned to the VIP room went and got new airline t-shirts for Phillie and Jennifer. After Marie and I had time to clean our children and ourselves in the washroom, I decided to call my mom and let her know what had happened to us.

My mom asked me if we had called Marie's family yet and I told her, "No, Marie wanted to wait until we talked to you first."

Mom said; "Don't tell anyone else anything until you get back home with us."

Up until this time I didn't realize who was behind all this.

I said, "Marie do you think that your father had something to do with this?"

She said, "Yes."

We started to speculate that he called Uncle Sammy to get someone to do this to us. I was in total disbelief. Dads don't do this to their children and grandchildren. If they did, they don't do this to people outside of their family, like me. Years later, there was this horrible bumper sticker that said something like this. "If you love something, set it free and if it doesn't come back hunt it down and kill it." I think that my father-in-law, the "old devil," inspired that one.

We pulled into Philadelphia Airport and the undercover cops were all over the place. My eyes were literally wide open. My senses were on high alert. I was able to see everything that was out of the norm. Your judgment and reaction are not what it should be but you are keen to your surroundings. It seems to me that fear shrinks your brain. In that state, your brain tells your body to be ready to do things out of the norm and focus on one thing, survival.

It seemed as if my entire family was there to meet us. The first thing I said to my mom and dad was, "I think Marie's father is trying to kill us." Neither my mom nor my dad said anything in response.

The next three nights we stayed at my siblings' homes. The first night we stayed with Katherine, Wayne, Donna, and their new baby girl, Denise. I took a shower and tried to get a good night's sleep. When I awoke, Marie was downstairs answering questions from my family. That evening we celebrated Jennifer's first birthday with cake and ice cream. It was surreal.

The next night we stayed down in Delaware at my sister Ann's place. It was at this time we were supposed to be in San Francisco. We didn't want to call her house directly because the old man liked to listen to everyone's phone conversation and he may prompt them into asking too many questions. Instead,

Marie called her brother Anthony. She told him that everything is fine and we are staying at the Holiday Inn next to the San Francisco Airport.

The next night, we stayed at my brother, James's place with his wife and their daughter, Summer. It was time to try again. I called my brother John and asked if he would give us a ride out to California. He was just out of the Army and had not found a job yet. He said that he would, but not to San Francisco. He wanted to go to San Diego because Alice Carr was living there and she wanted him to come out to visit her.

And that's what we did. James loaned me his .38 caliber handgun and we collected some money from my family. So with about two hundred and eighty dollars we all piled into my brother John's 1967 yellow Plymouth Duster and headed for California. We headed south on Interstate 95 and turned right in Virginia to I-85 and hopped on the I-40 west. We didn't stop except for gas, food, and restrooms until we passed Tulsa, Oklahoma. John drove all the way until we stopped late one night in Oklahoma City. It was a roadside motel and the only vacancy they had was the honeymoon suite. I didn't care that the room was all red with this heart-shaped bed encircled by pleated curtains and a mirror on the ceiling.

John was grossed out by it and said, "I'm not staying here with my brother and his wife and two kids." I was at my wit's end and I didn't care where we slept just as long as it was clean and safe. I just laughed and flopped on the bed and went to sleep. John went back to the office and demanded another room and they gave it to us. I got up one more time and moved to another room before falling asleep. The next day, as we were crossing the desert, I was wondering if perhaps my son's "Id" had been violated beyond repair. Jennifer, my daughter, a flower I must nourish and preserve for another-would that be too hard to do? My brother John, what could I ever do to repay him? And Marie, my wife, a purple carnation nourished by dark water, could she withstand the change?

So after three days of driving, we made it to the California State line. It was only a sign, but to us, it was a place where we could put our children to bed in peace and we could rest. So, as thousands of couples before us, I leaned over to my wife and kissed her on the lips. And said, "Marie, I think we are going to be able to make it here."

She replied, "I think you're right, Phillip."

THE · END

A Couple of Nobodies...

CPSIA information can be obtained
at www.ICGtesting.com
Printed in the USA
LVHW050756161120
671800LV00001B/111